12 LEADERSHIP LESSONS from the LIFE of CHRIST

12 LEADERSHIP LESSONS from the LIFE of CHRIST

KIMBALL FISHER

Plain Sight Publishing
An Imprint of Cedar Fort, Inc.
Springville, Utah

ISBN 13: 978-1-4621-1799-4

Published by Plain Sight, an imprint of Cedar Fort, Inc.
2373 W. 700 S., Springville, UT 84663
Distributed by Cedar Fort, Inc., www.cedarfort.com

LIBRARY OF CONGRESS CATALOGING-IN-PUBLICATION DATA

Names: Fisher, Kimball, author.
Title: 12 leadership lessons from the life of Jesus Christ / Kimball Fisher.
Other titles: Twelve leadership lessons from the life of Jesus Christ
Description: Springville, Utah : Plain Sight Publishing, An imprint of Cedar
    Fort, Inc., [2016] | Includes bibliographical references and index. |
    Description based on print version record and CIP data provided by
    publisher; resource not viewed.
Identifiers: LCCN 2015048472 (print) | LCCN 2015048086 (ebook) | ISBN
    9781462117994 (epub, pdf, mobi) | ISBN 9781462117994 (perfect bound : alk.
    paper)
Subjects: LCSH: Leadership--Religious aspects. | Jesus Christ--Leadership.
Classification: LCC BL65.L42 (print) | LCC BL65.L42 F57 2016 (ebook) | DDC
    158/.4--dc23
LC record available at http://lccn.loc.gov/2015048472

Cover design by Krystal Wares
Cover design © 2016 by Cedar Fort, Inc.
Edited and typeset by Rebecca Bird

Printed in the United States of America

10 9 8 7 6 5 4 3 2 1

Printed on acid-free paper

For my life and work partner, Mareen Fisher,
who is the most Christlike leader I know.

CONTENTS

CONTENTS

ACKNOWLEDGMENTS

I would like to thank the wonderful team at Cedar Fort for their invaluable assistance on this project. Special thanks to my editor Chelsea Jackson and copyeditor/interior designer Rebecca Bird for making this a better, more readable book. Thanks, too, to Krystal Wares for the awesome cover design and to Brantz Woolsey for some great marketing support.

As always, I couldn't have done this book without the research, writing, and emotional assistance of my talented wife and business partner, Mareen. Thanks, sweetheart. I'd also like to express my gratitude to my Organizational Behavior professors (many of whom I've quoted in this book) for being both extraordinary leadership scholars and exemplars of Christlike values. My special appreciation goes to Steve Covey, Gene Dalton, Bill Dyer, Kate Kirkham, Bonner Ritchie, Paul Thompson, Alan Wilkins, and Warner Woodworth. Although I'm saddened by the loss of several of these mentors, I'm confident that heaven has better leaders as a result of their transfers.

AUTHOR'S NOTE

After I wrote a book entitled *The Christlike Leader* (Springville, Utah: Cedar Fort, 2015) for my own faith community, I received several requests to do a similar project for a more general audience. Although this volume is primarily original, it contains some material from the earlier work.

The book uses the standard King James English translation of the Bible.

INTRODUCTION

The simplest definition of a leader is someone who has followers. Using this measure of leadership effectiveness, it's pretty easy to make an argument that with more than two billion followers,[1] the greatest leader of all time may be Jesus Christ. But the current disfavor of religion in many societal and organizational settings has discouraged the popular consideration of his leadership practices. I think that's a shame.

For the majority of the last three decades, I have worked with about twenty percent of the Fortune 100 corporations—places like Apple Computers, Bristol-Myers Squibb, Capital One, Chevron, GE Capital, Hewlett-Packard, Intel, McDonald's, Microsoft, NBC, Nike, and Weyerhaeuser—teaching leadership skills across America, Europe, Scandinavia, Asia, and Africa. I've also worked with government clients such as the IRS, the U.S. Departments of Treasury and Agriculture, and the Staff Office of the U.S. Senate on the same topics. It's been a wonderful career. I've enjoyed my consulting and training engagements helping managers and executives learn techniques and perspectives that improve leadership effectiveness. But few have realized that many of the principles and practices of leadership that we consider to be the leading-edge thinking on the subject—for example, servant-leadership, visionary messaging techniques, and group motivation theory—are over two thousand years old. Ripples from the revolutionary leadership principles taught in the stories of the New Testament have washed across the entire earth for centuries. However, they still have not completely displaced the largely dysfunctional traditional management practices from the onset of the Industrial Revolution or the pervasive aristocratic leadership thinking that predates Christ.

I understand the reluctance that many people may have for considering the leadership practices of the great religious teachers—virtually all of whom have spawned some radicalized sects who have harassed or even terrorized others with their beliefs. But this omission—however well founded—results in the unfortunate loss of opportunity for the improved leadership of our organizations, schools, communities, and countries. If we can learn ways to better lead our organizations, shouldn't we?

I confess to a certain bias on these matters. I was raised in a religious home and continue to actively practice my faith. I've known the stories I'll share in this book from the time I was very young. And I believe my long association with them offers me a unique perspective—and hopefully some useful insights—that a dispassionate leadership consultant or researcher may not have. To this end, I ask you to keep an open mind and honestly consider whether the leadership practices presented in the New Testament could help you become more effective—regardless of whether or not you consider yourself religious, let alone Christian.

It may help you to know that I am not alone in recommending these practices. No less than management guru Ken Blanchard of *The One Minute Manager* fame[2] and respected Harvard-trained leadership scholar Charles Manz[3] have published important books about the leadership practices of Jesus Christ. I sincerely hope you will find my take on the topic helpful as well. I'd like to introduce you to what I believe are a dozen essential leadership lessons from the stories of his life.

NOTES

1.   Wikipedia, "List of Religious Populations" accessed January 7, 2016, https://en.wikipedia.org/wiki/List_of_religious_populations.

2.   Ken Blanchard and Phil Hodges, *Lead Like Jesus* (Nashville: Thomas Nelson, 2005).

3.   Charles Manz, *The Leadership Wisdom of Jesus* (San Francisco: Berrett-Kohler, 1998).

Where there is no vision, the people perish. (Proverbs 29:18)

LESSON 1
BE VISIONARY

One of the leadership practices from the great religious traditions that has received wide acceptance for its obvious utility is the concept of visionary leadership. A leader's vision of a desirable future is highly motivating and encourages people to work hard, make good choices, sacrifice, and continuously improve. This is the first essential tool of leadership. While management skills are essential to operate and maintain the status quo, it is the tools of leadership—especially vision—that are essential to creating the highest levels of commitment and extraordinary results. If you want your organization to run smoothly, then stay within policy guidelines, meet budgets and time commitments, and use good management skills. But if you need *more*, such as the extraordinary effort to turn around a struggling operation during challenging times; the creation of innovative practices, processes, products, and services that haven't been invented yet; or the highest levels of creativity, enthusiasm, and loyalty, consider doing what Jesus Christ did.

A MOTIVATING VISION OF A DESIRABLE FUTURE ENCOURAGES PEOPLE TO:

- Work hard
- Make sacrifices
- Continuously improve

Figure 1-1: The Power of Vision

CHRIST AS A VISIONARY LEADER

People followed Jesus Christ because he preached about the kingdom of God—a place so much better than the Roman-occupied territories where they lived. They found the idea both inspiring and liberating. While Jesus Christ normally spoke of a kingdom that was not of this world, the vision of a place of peace where all were accepted, loved, treated fairly, and rewarded based on merit rather than birthright or affiliation was so compelling that throngs of people regularly crowded to hear him. His vision challenged the status quo, made it seem insufficient, and motivated people to take action to change themselves and their situation. As we read in the gospel of Luke: "And the people . . . followed him: and he received them, and spake unto them of the kingdom of God" (Luke 9:11) and "the people sought him, and came unto him, and stayed him, that he should not depart from them [but] . . . he said unto them, I must preach the kingdom of God to other cities also: for therefore am I sent" (Luke 4:42–43).

The authorities of his day saw his rapidly growing power base of highly dedicated followers as a threat to their way of life, and eventually to their form of government, despite his explanations: "And when he was demanded of the Pharisees, when the kingdom of God should come, he answered them and said, The kingdom of God cometh not with observation: Neither shall they say, Lo here! or, lo there! for, behold, the kingdom of God is within you" (Luke 17:20–21). Even though authorities lacked convicting evidence, the power of Christ's vision to amass followers over his three-year ministry made the political and religious leaders nervous. They feared open rebellion. So, they engaged in the mockery of a false trial and quickly executed him.

KEY ELEMENTS OF A VISION

Through vision, leaders identify specific opportunities for significant improvement. Christ, of course, was a sterling example of this. But we have records of visionary leaders that predate Jesus. For example, in the Pentateuch—the first five books of the Old Testament, which are also found in both the Torah and the Koran—the prophet Moses led the children of Israel out of bondage in Egypt in accordance with his vision of taking them to a promised land.

Like Moses, visionary leaders help people see an alternative to their present situation that requires their special effort to achieve a promised land. But unlike Moses, a visionary leader normally helps people move not from one geographical spot to another one, but from one state of being to another: from ineffectiveness to effectiveness, for example, or from disorganization to organization, or from non-productivity to productivity.

Leaders invite people to leave their own personal or organizational Egypt to journey to a land of great future promise. We've worked with leaders in a forest products company, for example, who turned around a struggling lumber business with a vision of creating affordable homes. The leaders communicated this vision by taking groups of employees out on service projects to build homes for the homeless with Habitat for Humanity. The employees who had been unimpressed with previous leaders' visions for "reduced cost" felt a special bond with the people they met who would be unable to purchase a home without the help of charity—unless their company's dimensional lumber became less expensive.

Regardless of the type of journey, however, a visionary leader helps his or her followers identify three key points illustrated in Moses's story. First, people must know the envisioned destination. Second, they must understand where they are now and why it is important to leave the comfort of the known way of being. Third, they must understand how to get from here to there. For example, when Christ spoke of the kingdom of God, the authorities became threatened because he spoke of a desirable place clearly different than Rome-occupied Israel. This clearly articulated future state created dissatisfaction with current events (many business leaders now call this a disruption). It also illustrated the pathway from the current state to the future state by observance of the way of life Christ taught.

A GOOD VISION CREATES:

1. A clearly defined future state
2. A need to change from the current state
3. A high level roadmap of how to get to the future state from the current state

Figure 1-2: The Essential Attributes of Vision

When done properly, a clear and compelling vision can motivate and inspire others to accomplish remarkable things. Many historians, for example, claim that advances in race relations in the United States, as well as putting the first astronaut on the moon, resulted largely from the visionary leadership of Dr. Martin Luther King Jr.[1] and President John F. Kennedy,[2] respectively. Two thousand years later, Christ's vision about his father's kingdom still motivates more than two billion followers.

In each case, the visionary leader frequently and powerfully explained the envisioned destination. He shared examples of how the current reality fell short of the vision, and he shared ideas about how to get from here to there. This is job number one of the leader. Leading. You might even say that the definition of leading is generating the vision that will create a high level of commitment to executing objectives and plans for organizational improvement. Managers maintain organizations, and that's important, but it is different from leading. Leaders transform organizations.

A VISIONARY LEADER:

1. Generates and communicates a compelling vision
2. Creates high levels of commitment to the vision
3. Helps people develop and execute objectives and plans to accomplish the vision

Figure 1-3: Visionary Leadership Essentials

MEANS VISIONS VERSUS ENDS VISIONS

After a vision is shared, there is an additional benefit. Prioritization of activities can then happen on many levels. The activities that are contrary to the vision can be eliminated. The things we are doing that help us accomplish the mission can be maintained. Then we can determine which of our activities are more useful to the accomplishment of the vision.

The visioning process appears to have a sequence. If leaders start with the envisioned destination (ends), they are able to trim down the change requirements (means) to only the most critical items. Less visionary leaders, however, generally start with the means. These types of visions have at least two problems. First, "means" visions seldom motivate. The previously mentioned example of the wood products company vision illustrates this point. The originally stated vision to "reduce cost" was more of a means vision than an ends vision. It answered the question "what should we work on?" but not "why should we work on it?" Understandably, it lacked the power to inspire people to the highest levels of motivation because employees naturally assumed that once their efforts to reduce costs had been accomplished, it would probably result in nothing more than increased profitability for the company and higher management bonuses. While that vision may have been inspiring to managers, it lacked the power and clarity to create enthusiasm in the troops. The "ends" vision of helping every child be able to afford a house, however, did the trick.

STEPS TO CREATING A VISION:

1. Define the end state, then
2. Define the key means required to reach the end state
Warning: Don't define potential means until the end is clear!

Figure 1-4: Vision Development Sequence

Means visions have another weakness as well. They often create a proliferation of activities, meetings, and programs that while often good, are not the best use of time for either the leader or for those within his or her stewardship. As a rule of thumb, the visionary leader is reluctant to add any activity that isn't motivated by a clearly inspired vision that benefits those he or she serves and clearly leads to the envisioned destination.

MEANS VISIONS

- Focuses on methods or techniques
- Answers "how?"
- Inspires low motivation
- Defines one pathway
- Generates activities
- Hurts prioritization

ENDS VISIONS

- Focuses on transformation
- Answers "why?"
- Inspires high motivation
- Allows multiple pathways
- Generates commitment
- Helps prioritization

Figure 1-5: Means Visions versus Ends Visions

One of the greatest challenges of modern leadership isn't how to create more things for people to do. It is, conversely, to help them eliminate part of the activity clutter that prevents them from being as productive as possible. The lumber company's vision to create affordable housing—especially because it was communicated so effectively—helped employees not only get excited about helping customers, it also focused their attention on the projects that were most useful to reducing the pricing of the most popular dimensional lumber products—2×4s. This focus allowed them to eliminate the less useful but time consuming activities that primarily reduced the costs of lesser-used materials.

VISION STATEMENTS

A vision statement is a useful tool for the visionary leader—it's a document that clarifies the general purpose and direction of an organization or initiative. I've seen this idea applied even in families. Some call them "family vision statements," and others call them "mission statements." They often include words such as: "our home will be a place of love and refuge from the world" or "we believe in wholesome family recreation—preferably on water!" or "we eat, pray, and laugh together," or simply "families are forever." These documents can serve the practical purpose of prioritizing the often overcrowded schedule of a typical family by simply providing an excuse for any family member to ask: "is the activity we are considering consistent with our vision or not?" If not, it is eliminated. This is an ancient idea that goes back at least as far as the prophet Joshua, who shared his family's vision statement when he declared: "As for me and my house, we will serve the Lord" (Joshua 24:15).

SUMMARY

As visionary leaders, we can move the work of our organizations forward by helping those within our stewardships understand how to reach a better future. We do this by helping them understand where they are, what it looks like to be somewhere better, and then how to get from here to there. This type of vision is not only an effective tool of leadership, but also an excellent method for prioritizing the flood of activities that often drown us in the modern world (leader and follower alike).

For more ideas about how to apply the lesson of visionary leadership to your own leadership responsibilities in your organization, community, and/or home, please refer to the appendix for potential projects. The appendix contains specific suggestions to help you apply each of the twelve lessons from the life of Jesus Christ.

In the next chapter we will review what it means to be a servant leader.

NOTES

1. Martin Luther King Jr., "I Have a Dream" (Washington DC: Lincoln Memorial), August 28, 1963.

2.   John F. Kennedy, "We Choose to Go to the Moon" (Houston, TX: Rice Stadium), September 12, 1962.

But Jesus called them unto him, and said, Ye know that the princes of the Gentiles exercise dominion over them, and they that are great exercise authority upon them. But it shall not be so among you: but whosoever will be great among you, let him be your minister; And whosoever will be chief among you, let him be your servant. (Matthew 20:25–27)

LESSON 2
BE A SERVANT LEADER

Since before the time of Christ, leadership was often more about obtaining, maintaining, and exercising power than anything else. Leaders were seen as inherently superior with a mandate to compel normally reluctant subordinates to productive action.

CONTROL VERSUS COMMITMENT

Harvard scholar Richard Walton called this idea of dominion the control paradigm, and he suggested that it has long been a pervasive perspective of leadership.[1] The idea is, in short, that many leaders still think their responsibility is to control others as suggested in the still repeated mantra taught in many MBA courses: the job of the manager is to plan, organize, direct, and control.[2]

Walton advises leaders to find a different paradigm to avoid the plethora of motivation and productivity problems associated with this type of thinking. He calls it "the commitment paradigm" and suggests that leaders shift their view away from the idea of controlling others to the idea of generating employee commitment instead. Employee commitment, of course, comes not from a boss telling someone what to do (exercising authority over them), but instead from a supportive leader helping the individual or team to get whatever they need to be successful (information, resources, training, coaching, and so on).

CONTROL	COMMITMENT
• Maximize rules	• Minimize rules
• External control focus	• Internal control focus
• Use hierarchy	• Use education
• Restrict information	• Share information
• Centralize power	• Distribute power
• Low levels of training	• High levels of training
• Leaders are bosses	• Leaders are coaches

Figure 2-1: Control versus Commitment Paradigm.
Adapted from The Fisher Group, Inc. Leadership Skills Training Program ©
All rights reserved.

A popular way to make this paradigm shift is to become what many have called "a servant leader." Jesus Christ taught this idea more than two thousand years ago: "And whosoever shall exalt himself shall be abased; and he that shall humble himself shall be exalted" (Matthew 23:12). And: "If any man desire to be first, the same shall be last of all, and servant of all" (Mark 9:35).

SERVANT LEADERSHIP

When Anglican bishop Desmond Tutu received the Nobel Peace Prize in 1984 for his work with apartheid victims in South Africa, an interviewer asked him: "What, in your opinion, makes a good leader?" He answered: "I think ultimately you want a leader who is also a servant. I mean really the leader is a leader because he is a servant. . . . Nelson Mandela [who became President of South Africa following his incarceration and who in 1993 also won the prize] is someone who is not in it for his own aggrandizement. He leads on behalf of, for the sake of."[3] This is what Christ taught both in word and deed.

Jesus washed the feet of his apostles, a task seen at his time as being below the dignity of a leader. But by so doing, he demonstrated an alternative model of leadership. Instead of being viewed as better than those they lead, and often above the law (not subject to the same rules as the non-leaders), Christ taught that leaders should be examples of obedience to the law, and see themselves as servants to, rather than rulers over, those they lead. "If I then, your Lord and Master, have washed your feet; ye also ought to wash one another's feet. For I have given you an example, that ye should do as I have done to you. Verily, verily, I say unto you, The servant is not greater than his lord; neither he that is sent greater than he that sent him. If ye know these things, happy are ye if ye do them" (John 13:14–17).

The notion of hierarchy, often drawn on organizational charts as a pyramid, dictates that the "head" (notice the hierarchical language here) of an engineering or teaching department, for example, should "supervise" (because as the word indicates, they must have superior vision, intelligence, or position) the others in "their" (as though the bosses own the people) department. Individual contributors "report to" (should be directed by the boss and follow orders) their "superiors." Rank is often more important than contribution.

But as the apostle Paul so eloquently instructs, the servant leader views himself or herself as just one of the parts of the whole operation, all of which are essential, with no one more or less important that anyone else:

> For the body is not one member, but many. If the foot shall say, Because I am not the hand, I am not of the body; is it therefore not of the body? And if the ear shall say, Because I am not the eye, I am not of the body; is it therefore not of the body? If the whole body were an eye, where were the hearing? If the whole were hearing, where were the smelling? . . . And the eye cannot say unto the hand, I have no need of thee: nor again the head to the feet, I have no need of you. Nay, much more those members of the body, which seem to be more feeble, are necessary: And those members of the body, which we think to be less honourable, upon these we bestow more abundant honour; and our uncomely parts have more abundant comeliness. (1 Corinthians 12:14–17, 21–23)

When his frightened parents lost him in the Jerusalem crowds and then finally discovered Jesus teaching his "superiors" in the temple, they were understandably upset. This was not the place for a boy! Nor was that sort of behavior acceptable in a culture that espoused education, position, seniority, and social status above inexperience and youth. But Jesus gently explained that he was on an errand from God—an errand that required him to do things differently than the established traditions and practices of the secular world. He would later reinforce these differences by teaching: "Render therefore unto Cæsar the things which are Cæsar's; and unto God the things that are God's" (Matthew 22:21). The ideas of rank, hierarchy, social status, special privilege or perquisites associated with titles, and other organizational and social practices that imply that one person is more important than another may offer societies a sense of order, but they do not necessarily make more effective leaders. Christ taught: "Ye are they which justify yourselves before men; but God knoweth your hearts: for that which is highly esteemed among men is abomination in the sight of God" (Luke 16:15).

DOMINION LEADERSHIP	SERVANT LEADERSHIP
• Elicits compliance	• Engenders commitment
• Supervision is necessary	• Education is necessary
• Focuses on hierarchy	• Focuses on results
• Seldom trusts others	• Usually trusts others
• Hoards power	• Empowers others
• Gives orders	• Makes suggestions
• Suppresses deviance	• Encourages creativity
• Manages by policy	• Manages by principles
• Uses directives	• Uses boundary conditions
• Seen as superior	• Seen as equal
• Favors punishment processes	• Favors reward processes
• Believes in selective info sharing	• Believes in transparent info sharing
• Believes hierarchy should decide	• Believes non-hierarchy should decide
• Emphasis on means	• Emphasis on ends
• Rewards required improvement	• Rewards continuous improvement
• Encourages agreement	• Encourages thoughtful disagreement

Figure 2-2: Dominion versus Servant Leadership
Adapted from The Fisher Group, Inc. Leadership Skills Training Program © All rights reserved.

SERVANT LEADERSHIP COMPETENCIES

I've written elsewhere about a proposed model for servant leaders,[4] offering seven competency clusters that provide an alternative to the dominion leader idea still popular today. The seven competencies are leader, results catalyst, facilitator, barrier buster, business analyzer, coach, and living example. See Figure 2-3: Leader Competency Model for a brief description of the seven components.

THE SERVANT LEADER

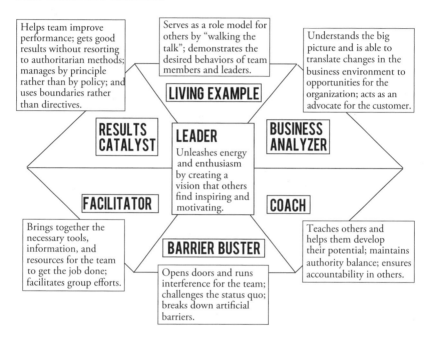

Helps team improve performance; gets good results without resorting to authoritarian methods; manages by principle rather than by policy; and uses boundaries rather than directives.

Serves as a role model for others by "walking the talk"; demonstrates the desired behaviors of team members and leaders.

LIVING EXAMPLE

Understands the big picture and is able to translate changes in the business environment to opportunities for the organization; acts as an advocate for the customer.

RESULTS CATALYST

LEADER
Unleashes energy and enthusiasm by creating a vision that others find inspiring and motivating.

BUSINESS ANALYZER

FACILITATOR

COACH

Brings together the necessary tools, information, and resources for the team to get the job done; facilitates group efforts.

BARRIER BUSTER

Opens doors and runs interference for the team; challenges the status quo; breaks down artificial barriers.

Teaches others and helps them develop their potential; maintains authority balance; ensures accountability in others.

Figure 2-3: Leader Competency Model

We can use this same approach to identify the servant leader competencies demonstrated by Jesus Christ. See Figure 2-4 to see my descriptions of his specific leadership approach.[5] Although some of these competencies are unique to the religious nature of his ministry, many of them are essential to all leadership assignments. Let's take a moment to explore how his leadership style can inform our responsibilities. As we discuss the competencies, we will also review the attributes commonly associated with Jesus Christ: virtue, temperance, godliness, knowledge, faith, hope, humility, righteousness, obedience, diligence, courage, patience, charity, and brotherly kindness (see Figure 2-5).

THE CHRISTLIKE LEADER

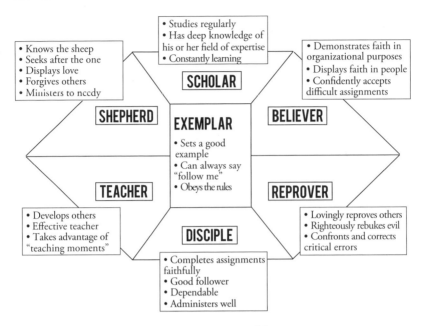

Figure 2-4: Christlike Leadership Competency Model
Adapted from The Christlike Leader.

EXEMPLAR

I believe that the core competency of Christ's leadership was to be an exemplar. Imagine if all leaders could honestly say as he did: "For I have given you an example, that ye should do as I have done to you" (John 13:15). Paul understood this when he told the Philippians: "Those things, which ye have both learned, and received, and heard, *and seen in me*, do: and the God of peace shall be with you" (Philippians 4:9; emphasis added).

The servant leader will also strive to emulate the attributes appropriate to this competency: virtue, temperance, and godliness. Don't be put off by the virtue of godliness. It means to be good, and even Christ rankled when people observed and commented on his goodness: "And Jesus said unto him, Why callest thou me good? none is good, save one, that is, God" (Luke 18:19).

SCHOLAR

Christ was also a scholar. He often quoted scripture, for example, as he taught those who followed him. And he gently criticized those who served as religious leaders who did not know or understand the writings of the prophets: "And Jesus answering said unto them, Do ye not therefore err, because ye know not the scriptures, neither the power of God?" (Mark 12:24).

His practice of regular scripture study, attendance at worship services, and personal devotion began early in his life and became a regular habit as indicated in Luke: "And he came to Nazareth, where he had been brought up: and, *as his custom was*, he went into the synagogue on the sabbath day, and stood up for to read" (Luke 4:16; emphasis added).

Following his example is essential if the organization you are leading is a religious one. But it is equally important to be a scholar in whatever learning is important to the operation you lead. Shouldn't a leader of a law firm know the law, or the leader of a technology business know both the business and the technology? Wouldn't it be wonderful for a government leader who claims to represent the viewpoints of his or her constituency to actually know the constantly evolving opinions and concerns of voters?

The Christlike attribute associated with this competency is knowledge, and the servant leader develops this knowledge by setting a personal example of regular and continuous study and learning.

BELIEVER

Jesus Christ was able to help others believe in the kingdom of God because he was a believer. He taught the gospel from his deep personal reservoir of faith and hope, the attributes associated with this competency. His faith was strong and began early in his life: "And the child grew, and waxed strong in spirit, filled with wisdom: and the grace of God was upon him" (Luke 2:40). He displayed faith and hope often by performing miracles.

Organizational leaders often need to display some little miracles, too. By demonstrating hope for a brighter future and faith in those they lead, they create positive energy and momentum. They help others accomplish things that often seem impossible, or miraculous, to the followers. And they truly believe in the organizations they lead. Nothing is more ineffective as leaders or more corrosive to the soul than a lack of commitment to the project, people, or purpose they serve. When servant leaders speak about an organizational value, direction, or initiative, others should be convinced that the leader believes what he or she is saying. And consistent with the core competency of being an exemplar, of course, the leaders' actions should *always* demonstrate their professed beliefs.

Sometimes when acting as leadership coaches, we ask a leader to write down their core beliefs: those fundamental values that direct their actions. Then we interview those they lead and ask, "What are your leader's core beliefs?" Unfortunately the lists aren't always the same. Why? Because as leaders we often judge ourselves on our intentions, while others judge us on what they actually see us do.

REPROVER

Jesus Christ displayed the humility necessary to seek out the will of his Father: "I seek not mine own will, but the will of the Father which hath sent me" (John 5:30). Jesus Christ humbly displayed the righteous conviction to reprove others when necessary. He firmly but lovingly corrected doctrines and behavior that he felt were incorrect. For example, he reproved sinners (see John 8:11), the chief priests and Pharisees (see Matthew 21:45–46), and his own apostles (see Matthew 14:31). In perhaps the only example of truly righteous indignation we ever see from him, he even made a small whip and drove out the animals, money changers, and merchants from the temple declaring, "Make not my Father's house an house of merchandise" (John 2:15).

The many stories of how he reproved Peter, whom he loved, are so instructive that I will discuss them throughout the book. I'll also devote a chapter (Lesson 10: Correct Others Properly) to exploring how we can properly follow the reproving example of Jesus Christ in our organizations and homes.

DISCIPLE

Jesus Christ was an example of discipleship: "I do nothing of myself; but as my Father hath taught me, I speak these things. And he that sent me is with me: the Father hath not left me alone; for I do always those things that please him" (John 8:28–29), and: "For I came down from heaven, not to do mine own will, but the will of him that sent me" (John 6:38).

The attributes he showed as a disciple were obedience and diligence, attributes that the servant leader also displays. He or she understands that part of being a leader is to be an effective follower.

TEACHER

Much of the record we have of Christ's life contains the content and method of his highly skilled teaching. He taught as one having authority, unlike the Pharisees and Sadducees of his day, and he used powerful techniques that servant leaders emulate. Rarely was his teaching critical, being primarily loving in tone. He used questions to cause people to think and parables or stories that adapted his messages to the lives and understanding of the learners. As a teacher he demonstrated the attributes of courage and patience. He took personal risks and wasn't afraid of how others might view him.

So we must, as modern leaders, teach at every appropriate opportunity. It is a powerful tool of leadership and essential to the development of others—as we will demonstrate in a later chapter dedicated to this subject. And courage is always required from leaders who wish to innovate or improve. It is often necessary to stand firm against the tide of popular belief, to withstand the social pressure of "the way we have always done things before," and to demonstrate the courageous conviction necessary to change an organizational culture—especially if that culture has a proven track record of previous success. It always takes courage to do what is right, despite how different from the norm it may be.

One of my favorite stories about Christ's teaching occurs, as already mentioned, when he is only twelve-years-old. We read of this experience: "And it came to pass, that after three days they found him in the temple, sitting in the midst of the doctors, both hearing them, and asking them questions. And all that heard him were astonished at his understanding and answers" (Luke 2:46–47). Imagine a twelve-year-old teaching the most learned scholars of his day. What courage and wisdom it must have taken. He would display this courageous and dynamic teaching skill his entire life.

SHEPHERD

One of the greatest competencies of servant leadership can be described as shepherding. Jesus is often called the good shepherd (John 10:11–14), the one who knows the names of the sheep and was known of them. He who would forsake the many to serve the one. His ministry of charity and brotherly kindness is an example to all who wish to be servant leaders. Paul encourages us to: "walk in love, as Christ also hath loved us, and hath given himself for us an offering and a sacrifice to God" (Ephesians 5:2).

Anyone who wants to lead as Jesus did will get to know those he or she serves, spend time with them, display love, and forgive their mistakes. You probably won't find that on a leader's job description in most organizations, but the loyalty and support generated from genuinely caring about others almost always creates remarkable returns. For example, I remember once working as a consultant to a company that was struggling with their union-management relations. One plant manager seemed to do better than most others. When I asked some union officers why they worked so hard to maintain positive relationships with this leader, one of them replied: "He hasn't missed the funeral of a direct family member of an employee in the last five years." In the terms of this chapter, that plant manager was clearly a shepherding leader, demonstrating concern for others—even when it required sacrificing his own precious weekends to do so.

CHRISTLIKE ATTRIBUTES

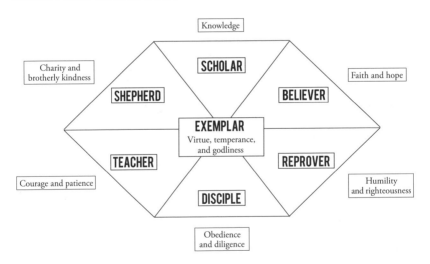

Figure 2-5: Christlike Attributes

SUMMARY

Understanding how servant leadership differs from popular dominion-type leadership notions in the world today can help us be more effective. The bottom line is this: leaders are to be servants to, not bosses over, those within their stewardships. They flip the traditional pyramid shaped organization chart upside down. Their behavior, organizational structures, and organizational policies serve not to control people, but to generate the highest potential level of commitment to self-control.

In the next chapter we will learn the critical importance of setting a good example for others—the core competency of servant leadership demonstrated by Jesus Christ. If we want to emulate his style of leading, we must be able to, as he did, consistently invite others to: "Come, follow me." The unspoken sermon of personal example is far more powerful than almost anything else a servant leader can communicate.

NOTES

1.   Richard Walton, "From Control to Commitment in the Workplace," *Harvard Business Review*, March/April 1985.

2.   Kimball Fisher, *Leading Self-Directed Work Teams* (New York: McGraw-Hill, 2000), 106–11.

3.   Desmond Tutu, "Desmond Tutu on Leadership," interview by Nobelprize.org, accessed on January 16, 2015, http://www.youtube.com.

4.   Fisher, *Leading Self-Directed Work Teams,* 134.

5.   Kimball Fisher, *The Christlike Leader* (Springville, UT: Cedar Fort, 2015).

For I have given you an example, that ye should do as I have done to you. (John 13:15)

LESSON 3
BE A GOOD EXAMPLE

The core competency of a Christlike leader is to set a good example. As Paul implored of those who professed to believe Jesus, "be thou an example of the believers, in word, in conversation, in charity, in spirit, in faith, in purity" (1 Timothy 4:12).

Christ's simple admonition to "Follow me" (Matthew 4:19, Matthew 16:24, Luke 9:59, John 1:43, John 12:26) is the most powerful illustration of personal example that I can think of in the history of leadership. He never asked someone to do something he wasn't willing to do himself. He put his leadership message in his actions, not just in his words. In contemporary management parlance he not only "talked the talk" but he "walked the walk." I can find no incident in the New Testament where he failed to do anything less than what he asked of his followers. And his moral authority came from his unwavering ability to do "the right thing" without deviation.

AN EXEMPLARY LEADER:

- Consistently sets a good example in all things
- Puts his or her key messages in his or her behavior
- Talks the talk and walks the walk
- Never asks anyone to do something he or she wouldn't (or preferably doesn't already) do
- Can, with moral authority, say: "follow me and do what I do"

Figure 3-1: The Attributes of an Exemplary Leader

"FOLLOW ME"

Rather than simply preaching forgiveness as an important virtue, for instance, he set a nearly incomprehensible example of forgiveness under the worst conceivable set of circumstances. As he hung on the wooden cross where the Romans had spiked his hands, wrists, and feet to torture and kill him by an agonizing and lengthy suffocation, there was no blaming of one of his best friends for the betrayal that would lead to his death, no complaint about his wrongful capture or illegal trial, nor any completely justifiable recrimination of the religious and civic leaders who had put his murder into motion. Rather, the words of Christ were: "Father, forgive them; for they know not what they do" (Luke 23:34).

POOR EXAMPLES

Conversely, as a personal leadership coach, I can't count the number of conversations I've had with individual managers that went something like this:

ME: "What do you need most from the people you lead?"

THEM: "To do their jobs well."

ME: "Could you be more specific?"

THEM: "Sure. For example, I really need Brandon (or Mohammed or Mei Ling or Anton) to be on time for meetings (or follow up with clients, get reports in on schedule, keep spending under the budget, generate ideas for new products/services, keep confidences). When he's late (or fails to follow up, meet schedule, overspends, doesn't innovate, doesn't keep confidences) he misses important information and the opportunity to participate in team decisions (or we lose clients, have costly schedule delays, lose money, become uncompetitive in the marketplace, lose trust)."

ME: "Have you talked with him (or her) about your expectations and concerns?"

THEM: "Several times. But he (or she) doesn't seem to think it's important."

ME: "Is there anything you could be doing, perhaps even unintentionally, that would make him (or her) believe his (or her) behavior isn't important?"

THEM: "I don't think so. I always tell them it is."

ME: "Do you show them?"

THEM: "What?"

ME: "Have you ever been late to a meeting (or failed to follow up with one of your clients, been late with a report, or spent what others might think is too much money, or failed to come up with an innovation, or broken a confidence)?"

THEM: "I guess so, but I'm a manager, not an individual contributor. I have different responsibilities than they do. Sometimes I have to be late to meetings because something more important came up (or I had a problem that preempted my ability to follow up with that client, or they didn't understand why that expenditure was necessary, or I ran out of time to solve that problem, or there were legal reasons why I had to break that confidence)."

ME: "Do you see how Brandon (or Mohammed or Mei Ling or Anton) might see your example and assume that if you can act that way he (or she) can, too?"

THEM: "I guess I've never thought about it that way."

Exemplars don't say to people, "You should (do this or that)," they invite them to join the leader in doing whatever "it" is. They don't say, for example, "You should tell the truth." They demonstrate honesty even when it is difficult or inconvenient. They don't say, "You need to communicate more effectively." They demonstrate what effective communication looks like. They don't just ask people to work together more effectively; they personally and genuinely set an example of using excellent social skills.

A MEMORABLE EXAMPLE TO ME

When I served as a missionary for my church in Hokkaido, Japan, the leader of my mission was a man named Kotaro Koizumi. He told us a story to illustrate this point about being a good example to others. The president of our church at that time, Spencer W. Kimball, was once visiting the congregation my leader had presided over in Hawaii. Just prior to an important meeting, Koizumi discovered that President Kimball was missing. Koizumi desperately searched for our senior church leader and eventually discovered him in the men's restroom cleaning the floor.

Perhaps President Kimball might have chosen to give a wonderful talk in the conference about the importance of caring for church buildings. Perhaps he could have sent out a written communication urging members to treat these facilities with the special respect due a house of worship. But no sermon or communication would have carried that message more powerfully into the heart of my mission president than seeing the elderly leader on his hands and knees in the restroom, humbly and quietly serving where service was needed.

That's how Jesus did it. Of course he taught with great power about compassion and mercy through parables and exhortation. But many of his greatest sermons were given in practice rather than in preaching. In these moments he didn't just teach the ten lepers, or those who would stone the adulteress, or the parents of a dead little girl, or the apostle who in frustration cut off the ear of his enemy. He taught everyone who reads the accounts in the New Testament.

Remember that we can set a good example in our imperfection, too. Leaders who are trying to be exemplars, for instance, are quick to apologize when they make mistakes. They can demonstrate what Jesus Christ would call genuine repentance for sins (the incorrect behavior)—even if the "sins" they confess may seem to be relatively small ones. I've heard several team members say, for example, that they really appreciated when a team leader said something such as, "I want to apologize for losing my temper this morning. You guys deserve better than that from me."

A STORY ABOUT GANDHI

As a final reinforcement for this lesson of Christlike leadership, I'd like to share a story about Mahatma Gandhi, the leader of the non-violent independence movement for India. I've read several versions of this experience on the Internet and have not been able to tell which, if any, of them, is accurate. In some accounts, for example, the child in the story is a boy and in others a girl. The time periods vary in almost every account. But I did compile a version that included the most common story elements that appeared multiple times. I reviewed my compilation with Gandhi's granddaughter, with whom I worked as a consultant. She said she had heard the story and believed it to be true, but could not verify the particulars.

It goes like this:

One day a parent who was distraught about her child's eating habits made an appointment to see Gandhi. His schedule was full, but after a few months, she was able to take her child to meet the great man.

"Bapu," the mother said (calling Gandhi by his nickname), "my child has the greatest respect for you. I am concerned that he is eating too much sugar, and I believe that if you asked him to stop eating it he would listen to you and change his ways. Would you do us this favor?"

Gandhi stood still for a moment and then answered, "You must come back in six months."

The mother was perplexed but respectful, and so she left and made arrangements to return with her son six months later. At that meeting she reminded the great man of her request. Gandhi smiled and turned to the boy.

"Young friend," Gandhi said. "Please listen to your mother. Sugar is not good for you. I think it would be a good idea for you to stop eating it."

"I will do it," the boy agreed.

"Thank you, Bapu," said the mother. "But I do not understand. We have traveled a great distance to see you. It has taken a lot of time and expense. And my son has been eating sugar since our first meeting. Why didn't you ask him to change his diet six months ago? This would have saved us time and money."

"Because," Gandhi said, "when you came to me six months ago, I could not ask him to stop eating sugar, because I was still eating sugar."

I love that story. Think of what a better place our organizations and communities would be if we all had absolute confidence that our leaders would hold themselves to the same or higher standard than they expect from us. Gandhi may not have been perfect, but like Jesus Christ, in this situation he led with the moral authority that comes from setting an example of integrity and being able to say to the boy, "Follow me. Do what I do."

SUMMARY

Jesus Christ was a "follow me" leader, not a "do what I tell you to do" one. If we want to emulate his leadership, we will put our key messages in our actions and not just in our words. The power of individual example is far greater than any other form of communication. As the old chestnut goes, "Actions speak louder than words."

In the next chapter we will review one of the more challenging and important tasks of a leader: how to inspire and motivate others.

There is no fear in love; but perfect love casteth out fear: because fear hath torment. He that feareth is not made perfect in love. (1 John 4:18)

LESSON 4

BE INSPIRING AND MOTIVATING

I still remember a course at Brigham Young University (BYU) that Mareen and I took on the subject of motivation. On the first day of the graduate school class, the professor welcomed us and proclaimed, "The answer to the question 'how do you motivate people?' is that you can't!" I remember thinking, "Great. Why did I sign up for this course?" The professor then said something that I have reflected on for years. "The reason that you can't motivate people is that people have to motivate themselves. The best a leader can do is create an environment in which people feel inspired to do it."

MOTIVATION TIP #1:

Leaders can't motivate people. Leaders can only create an environment in which people are more likely to motivate themselves.

Figure 4-1: Key Motivation Tip #1

Glen Tucket, a former baseball coach and athletic director at BYU, explains this important principle this way: "We're now in an era of motivation. Everything we hear about is motivation this and motivation that. After we conclude a great [church] conference, people come up to me and say, 'Oh, didn't the speakers at conference motivate you?' I don't mean to be sacrilegious or anything, but my answer to them is, 'No, they didn't motivate me at all, but they surely inspired me to motivate myself.'"[1]

So how do we as leaders inspire others to motivate themselves? I'd like to suggest two crucial things Jesus Christ did in addition to the visionary leadership tips suggested in the first chapter: 1) ask good questions, and 2) love the people you are leading.

THE TWO KEY MOTIVATION TOOLS ARE:

1. Questions
2. A genuine concern for the people you lead

Figure 4-2: Key Tools of Motivation

ASK GOOD QUESTIONS

Before becoming a consultant, I worked as a manufacturing manager in a remarkable Procter & Gamble soap plant located in Lima, Ohio. We were organized into self-directed work teams with extraordinary levels of employee decision-making and problem solving. Our leaders believed it accounted for why our operation outperformed similar ones in P&G by 30 percent to 50 percent on virtually every business indicator. Why did it work so well? Partly because in the other plants, employees implemented *their manager's decisions*, but in Lima, employees mostly implemented *their own decisions*. It's hard not to get motivated by your own ideas.

MOTIVATION TIP #2:

Involve others in decision-making and problem solving. People always find their ideas more motivating than your ideas.

Figure 4-3: Key Motivation Tip #2

I soon concluded that questions were a powerful way to unleash this discretionary effort and self-motivation of others. When a problem occurred in our operation, for example, even though I was often tempted to tell the team members what I thought they should do to fix it, my manager had taught me to ask a series of questions that would help the team members solve the problem themselves. I'd ask questions such as "How did you first notice there was a problem?" or "Where have you run into this before?" or "How should we involve the plant engineer?" or "How should we fix this?" This did a few things. First, it reinforced that it was their responsibility to resolve the situation and not just identify that a problem had occurred. Second, it demonstrated my trust in their capabilities. Third, it helped them generate their own ideas about what to do. And when we used their ideas—even if their ideas didn't work—the team members were so motivated to make them work that they would usually modify their original but sub-optimal solutions continuously until the problem was solved. If they were only executing management ideas, however, they were more likely to say, "well, my boss's idea didn't work," and give up after the first failure.

Experts call this phenomenon "ownership." If you want to see a demonstration of ownership in action, drive by a block or two of rental homes and then drive by a block or two of homes that people own (even if, technically, the homes are still owned by a bank that people are making monthly payments to). Compare the way the rental homes look and are cared for to the way the owned homes are cared for. There are always exceptions, of course, but generally speaking you will see that the pride of ownership displayed in the resident-maintenance of owned properties is far superior to the resident-maintenance displayed in rented ones. Creating situations where people feel this pride of ownership motivates them to take action. Asking the right questions is a good way to do it.

SOCRATIC COACHING

People tell us that one of the most powerful and practical techniques we teach in our leadership training is a simple idea called Socratic coaching: asking questions to coach or correct instead of just giving advice or prescriptions for action. Instead of saying, "Carl, you need to be more organized in meetings," the leader says, "Carl, what is your agenda for the next meeting?" Asking the question puts the responsibility squarely on Carl's shoulders, not yours. It gets him to start thinking about solutions, not excuses, and inspires him to motivate himself to act differently.

Over the twenty years of teaching this technique, however, we have observed that some types of questions are better than others. Asking open-ended questions, such as "What is your plan?" for example, is far more effective than asking closed questions—questions that can be answered with a simple "yes" or "no," such as "Do you have a plan?" The reason is obvious. Engaging someone in a conversation allows the leader to discuss, encourage, and develop. A closed question does just exactly what it implies. It closes the conversation.

Another type of problematic question is one that implies criticism such as "Why did you do that?" or "What were you thinking?" For example, many years ago when I served as a scoutmaster for the Boy Scouts of America, I found that when the boys had made significant mistakes, it was much more useful to ask something such as, "What did you learn from that experience?" and hold my tongue when critical thoughts intruded. My patience was usually rewarded. They would talk about their mistakes openly and teach their peers about preparedness, or fire safety, or proper food preparation at the same time. Conversely, criticism questions, especially when asked publically, cause people to withdraw, close down, hang their heads, or get angry and defensive.

JESUS CHRIST ASKED GOOD QUESTIONS

Christ used questions masterfully. Let's look at some examples. He once asked his disciples: "Whom do men say that I the Son of man am?" (Matthew 16: 13). They answered: "Some say that thou art John the Baptist: some, Elias; and others, Jeremias, or one of the prophets" (Matthew 16:14) Then Christ asked the question again: "He saith unto them, But whom say *ye* that I am?" (Matthew 16:15; emphasis added). Peter answered: "Thou art the Christ, the Son of the living God" (Matthew 16:16).

A quick read of this incident might suggest that these questions were just an expression of Christ's casual curiosity. But by asking the questions, he did far more. He gave the disciples the opportunity to develop their own budding commitment to the cause—the motivating power required for action. His questions made his disciples think, evaluate their personal commitment, and motivate themselves to be stronger in their personal determination to building God's kingdom as preached by their leader.

MORE QUESTIONS FROM CHRIST

Jesus Christ used this method of asking questions to inspire motivation many times. In Matthew 20, for example, we read, starting with the verse 30: "And, behold, two blind men sitting by the way side, when they heard that Jesus passed by, cried out, saying, Have mercy on us, O Lord, thou Son of David" (Matthew 20:30). Surely Christ knew why they were calling for him. Crowds thronged him at this point of his ministry asking to be healed. If Matthew, his disciple who wrote the account, could tell that the two men were blind and infer that they wanted to be healed, couldn't Jesus also? But still he asks the question: "What will ye that I shall do unto you?" (Matthew 20:32).

He asked a question he already knew the answer to for *their* benefit, not his. Perhaps it was to inspire them to articulate their faith, a personal belief in the possibility of a miracle. Christ taught that faith was a necessary prerequisite to the healing process. "They say unto him, Lord, that our eyes may be opened. So Jesus had compassion on them, and touched their eyes: and immediately their eyes received sight, and they followed him" (Matthew 20:33–34).

Many times after performing these miracles, Christ said: "Thy faith hath made thee whole" (See Matthew 9:22, Mark 5:34, Luke 17:19, Mark 10:52, Matthew 15:28, Luke 8:48). Isn't asking the question of the blind men a way to motivate them to have a similar healing experience? (And please notice how you stop and think when I ask a question. Well-worded questions help you draw your own conclusions instead of merely accepting mine.)

Christ also used questions to teach and inspire action when he fed the five thousand. Read this passage carefully: "When Jesus then lifted up his eyes, and saw a great company come unto him, he saith unto Philip, Whence shall we buy bread, that these may eat? And this he said to prove him: *for he himself knew what he would do*" (John 6:5–6; emphasis added). The purpose of the question was to benefit Philip, not Jesus. Christ already knew what he was going to do, but he wanted to provide a way to strengthen Philip's faith by having him participate in a miracle.

Consider a final example. When Jesus reached out his hand to save Peter from drowning after Peter had tentatively accepted an invitation to walk on water, Jesus said: "O thou of little faith, wherefore didst thou doubt?" (Matthew 14:31). What sounds like a chastisement is, I believe, something much more. If his intention had been to shame Peter, Christ only needed to say something like, "I'm disappointed in you." But instead, he asked a question. He wanted to inspire Peter to action, to have him become motivated to reflect on the incident, to learn something, and to do better in the future.

Whether or not you believe that Christ performed the healings and miracles mentioned above, it is clear that one of the tools he used to motivate people to do remarkable things—things that they considered miraculous—was to ask questions. The New Testament account reports, for example, that Peter was later motivated to perform many of the same miracles as Jesus, including healings and the raising of the dead. According to the teachings of Christ, these behaviors would have been impossible without the faith Jesus questioned Peter about during Peter's failed attempt to walk on water.

LOVE OTHERS

The final way to help people motivate themselves is to love them. Several passages, for example, show how love motivated Christ himself.

CHRIST WAS MOTIVATED BY LOVE

Christ's love of his Father motivated him personally to obey the commandments: "If ye keep my commandments, ye shall abide in my love; even as I have kept my Father's commandments, and abide in his love" (John 15:10). And from his love of others, he motivated himself to heal the sick, raise the dead, and be crucified. As John writes about his death: "Greater love hath no man than this, that a man lay down his life for his friends" (John 15:13). The followers of Christ believed that Jesus willingly allowed himself to be killed because his death was a necessary sacrifice to help others.

CHRIST LOVED NON-SELECTIVELY

Remarkably, Christ's love for others was non-selective. He healed the ungrateful lepers as well as the grateful one. He even healed the severed ear of the soldier who had come to the Garden of Gethsemane to wrongfully incarcerate him.

The civic and religious leaders of his day criticized him for loving all types of people: "And when the scribes and Pharisees saw him eat with publicans and sinners, they said unto his disciples, How is it that he eateth and drinketh with publicans and sinners?" (Mark 2:16). But Jesus taught in both word and deed to "love one another, as I have loved you" (John 13:34 and 15:12), meaning, at least in part, that his followers should love not just people who were different than them, but even their avowed enemies as well. As Luke recorded, Jesus taught: "But I say unto you which hear, Love your enemies, do good to them which hate you" (Luke 6:27).

LOVE CASTETH OUT FEAR

Why is love such a powerful motivating force? Part of the answer is found in 1 John 4:18: "There is no fear in love; but perfect love casteth out fear: because fear hath torment. He that feareth is not made perfect in love" (1 John 4:18).

Edwards Deming was a quality guru and statistician who is often credited with the explosively successful Japanese economy following World War II. In his classic management book *Out of Crisis*, he taught that a key to productivity was the elimination of fear.[2] It is the eighth of his famous fourteen points. When employees, for example, fear that they will be punished for making a mistake, they will not be able to motivate themselves to take action except in the least risky set of circumstances. They choose inaction over action, avoid innovation and creativity, and hide mistakes instead of learning from them. So how can leaders drive out fear?

The leadership example of Jesus Christ suggests that the answer is love.

When we feel loved, the fear of recrimination decreases. Our fear of failure decreases. Love drives out other fears as well: the fear of rejection, the fear of isolation, the fear of manipulation, the fear of uselessness, the fear of loneliness, the fear of shame. Love breeds hope, optimism, and faith. It makes us feel that it is possible for us to do better. The love must be the pure type of love described in the first epistle of Peter: "Seeing ye have purified your souls in obeying the truth through the Spirit unto unfeigned love of the brethren, see that ye love one another with a pure heart fervently" (1 Peter 1:22). This passage reinforces a critical point about using love as a tool of motivation. If the concern for others is feigned (i.e., pretended) and employed only as a technique to inspire people to motivate themselves, it won't work. Love must be genuine to drive away fear.

CAN CHRISTLIKE LOVE BE USED IN SECULAR SETTINGS?

I've taught these motivational principles to hard-nosed leaders in businesses, unions, and government organizations for many years. I can't, of course, speak of Jesus Christ, or use the scriptures, since our clients forbid it. But a good results-oriented manager understands truth when he or she hears it. And ironically it is often this genuine concern for others that allows a Christlike leader to do some of the most difficult things required in secular settings.

I had to terminate someone once, for example, while working in a large corporation. These discussions can often be painful and emotional as a leader informs someone that they no longer have a job. But in this particular situation, the employee threw her arms around my neck and thanked me after I let her go. I believe that the reason was that I had shown her over the months that I had tried to help her make the improvements necessary to keep her job and that I genuinely wanted her to succeed. I attempted to show that I cared. And the truth is that I did. When it became painfully obvious to her that this job was not a good fit for her skills and aspirations (and after she knew that she had been given every chance to succeed), she understood that the decision to fire her had been made out of love and respect rather than something else.

SUMMARY

Technically, a leader is unable to motivate anyone to do anything. But a Christlike leader who asks good questions and genuinely loves others, can inspire those within his or her stewardship to motivate themselves to achieve their full potential.

In the next chapter we will review how a Christlike leader might work with groups of people.

NOTES

1. Glen Tucket, "Making Decisions and Feeding Sheep," *New Era,* January 1984, accessed March 16, 2015, http://www.lds.org.

2. William Edwards Deming, *Out of Crisis* (Boston: MIT Press, 2000). See chapter three.

And he said unto them, The kings of the Gentiles exercise lordship over them. . . . But ye shall not be so: but he that is greatest among you, let him be as the younger; and he that is chief, as he that doth serve. (Luke 22:25–26)

LESSON 5
EMPOWER TEAMS

As you probably know, teams, or what were sometimes anciently called "councils," operate differently than the traditional autocratic organizations criticized by Christ in the scripture that opens this chapter. Councils are highly participatory. Their strength comes from the collective wisdom and experience of many people, instead of a singular leader. In this chapter I'll introduce eight leadership tips for working effectively with teams. These tips will serve as an outline for most of the remaining chapters of the book. Therefore, in order to eliminate redundancy (and keep the book short enough that you'll want to read it), I will only briefly introduce the appropriate stories in the New Testament that will be discussed in far more detail in later chapters.

EMPOWERING TEAM LEADERS:

1. Facilitate, don't dominate
2. Encourage participation
3. Don't micromanage
4. Summarize and clarify
5. Drive discussions to action
6. Follow up
7. Support team members
8. Praise accomplishments

Figure 5-1: Eight Tips for Empowering Teams

EIGHT TIPS FOR MAKING TEAMS MORE EFFECTIVE

Teams can either be benefited if they follow or derailed if they fail to follow these few especially important leadership practices demonstrated by Jesus Christ.

TIP #1: FACILITATE, DON'T DOMINATE

Teams blossom under facilitative leaders who ask questions (as Christ did) and invite discussion instead of simply issuing orders and assignments. Although there are times when a Christlike leader may feel it is necessary to direct a specific course of action, these unilateral actions will normally occur only after a robust discussion of the issues at hand.

For example, rather than say, "We overspent this quarter, so please freeze all spending until further notice," the Christlike leader would say, "Let's counsel together about our financial situation. We overspent by 10 percent this quarter, and if this pattern continues we will run out of money a month before the year ends. What are your ideas about what we should do?" The first approach (what Christ called "lordship" and what leadership experts call "autocratic") is unilateral and fosters dependence on the leader. The second approach is multilateral. It fosters open discussion and self-reliance, and demonstrates trust. The best an autocrat can hope for is compliance. A Christlike leader wants to generate commitment.

Share problems, not solutions. When a leader exercises "lordship" over others, ownership is rare. Team members often drag their feet during implementation, wondering why the boss decided, for example, to freeze spending instead of eliminating a wasteful program. As a general rule of thumb, Christlike leaders are reluctant to dictate solutions because of this. As we recommend to our clients, "share the problem, not the solution." Sharing problems opens communication, helps team members better understand the complexity of the issues at hand, and increases higher levels of commitment to solving it. Sharing solutions closes discussion and limits team member participation to the implementation of someone else's idea based on that person's personal interpretation of the problem.

Consider an example to reinforce the point. When Christ met with those who wanted to stone the adulteress, he was certainly within his rights as a moral authority to command them to depart from the woman, thereby preventing a murder (although it was a legal killing under the law of the time). Instead of using the unilateral autocratic approach, however, what did he do? He said: "He that is without sin among you, let him first cast a stone at her" (John 8:7). In this case no group discussion was necessary to create a feeling of ownership for taking the correct course, and the scriptures report that each person present from the oldest to the youngest was "convicted by their own conscience" and left (John 8:9). This story is so packed with leadership learning that it will be used again to illustrate a variety of points. But one lesson it clearly teaches us is this: the most powerful way to generate commitment isn't to direct people. It is to create opportunities for them to direct themselves. They know what is right. But the Christlike leader has to exercise the patience and skill necessary to allow them to come to those conclusions on their own. Autocratic compulsion—even if it is polite or gentle—seldom accomplishes the highest level of performance.

TIP #2: ENCOURAGE PARTICIPATION

Although some members are eager to participate in teams, others require encouragement. A leader may, for example, have to invite a shy person to contribute to a discussion by asking something like: "Hans, you know more about this issue than any of us because you've been here longer. What do you think would be the best approach?" Jesus Christ often did this. For example, at the end of virtually every parable he taught, he asked the listener or listeners questions designed to help them draw their own conclusions. We will discuss in greater detail the method for inviting participation in lesson nine: "Be a Teacher."

In an attempt to create participation, however, avoid falling into the "round robin" trap. A round robin team meeting is one where all participants are assigned to do status reports every time. These routine reporting meetings can quickly devolve into mind-numbing sessions that leave insufficient time for prioritized future planning and problem-solving. They leave participants always looking in the rear view mirror instead of out of the windshield at the road ahead. You will crash.

TIP #3: DON'T MICROMANAGE

Sometimes in our anxiety to produce results, we claw back decision making and problem solving responsibilities from team members. This is often called "micromanagement" and it is highly detrimental to motivation, even if it is unintentional on the part of the leader. If someone, for example, is given an assignment to lead an activity and the leader swoops in and takes over, that person feels disempowered. He or she is unlikely to feel good about accepting responsibilities in the future, worried that his or her efforts may be hijacked or undermined by the leader. The same feeling comes when leaders make decisions that should rightly be made by others. Ironically, although the leader steps in and takes these actions to improve results, it will often do the opposite. The rightful decision maker will normally disengage, forcing the leader to continue assuming his or her responsibilities. We will speak of this thorny problem in more detail in a later chapter on delegation.

Muriel Maigan Wilkins, an executive coach, suggests that most micromanagers aren't even aware that they are doing it. But there are several warning signs. If you're "never quite satisfied with deliverables," or are often "frustrated because you would've gone about the task differently," or you "laser in on details and take great pride and/or pain in making corrections," "you ask for frequent updates," and you're constantly interested in "where all your team members are and what they're working on," you're a micromanager.[1] You're not alone. This is one of my personal challenges too. But there is an alternative approach.

For example, note that when Jesus Christ commissioned his leadership team of apostles, he gave them roles and responsibilities that were specific enough to provide direction without being so specific that they eliminated the opportunity for collective and individual interpretation (as we will also discuss in more detail in the chapter about delegation). Making assignments in this manner discourages micromanagement and forces the leader to manage more on results than methodology. Results focused leaders are less likely to limit participation in teams and more likely to empower.

TIP #4: SUMMARIZE AND CLARIFY

A valuable role that a leader can play in a team is to summarize and clarify council discussions and decisions. Although an effective meeting facilitator shouldn't dominate a meeting, he or she should help to keep it on track and on time. A good way to do this is to periodically summarize discussions by saying things such as: "We've heard some wonderful ideas about how to improve our relationship between the office and the field. It sounds like Mai's idea is to send two of the office people into the field for a six-week assignment. Is that right, Mai? What does everyone think about that?" A summary like this allows council members to support or disagree. It also drives the discussion to an appropriate conclusion.

Although we don't see Jesus Christ using this technique as often as the other methods we have discussed in this chapter, it is essentially what he did when he replied to the high priest attempting to trap him into a chargeable offense of blasphemy. Avoiding a direct answer of "yes, I am the Christ, the son of God" to the question of his accuser (perhaps to wisely avoid self-incrimination), he facilitated the discussion that was necessary to sentence himself to a death he believed was required of him. He offered this summarizing comment, "Thou hast said: nevertheless I say unto you, Hereafter shall ye see the Son of man sitting on the right hand of power, and coming in the clouds of heaven" (Matthew 26:64). His summary did provoke action. The high priest rent his garment, declared the guilt of Christ, and asked the crowd for their opinion. "They answered and said, He is guilty of death. Then did they spit in his face, and buffeted him; and others smote him with the palms of their hands" (Matthew 26: 66–67).

TIP #5: DRIVE DISCUSSIONS TO ACTION

As the previous tip suggests, having a discussion is only the first part of an effective facilitation. At some point the leader must ensure that some action is taken as a result. Christ displayed this technique in the assigning of the apostolic team to "feed my sheep" (preach about the kingdom of God) following a discussion with Peter about love and commitment to the cause (John 21:1–25).

You might say something such as: "We've agreed that we should invite the Sanchez family to the meeting next Wednesday evening. Maria could you do that this week and report back on Tuesday?" Or ask for a volunteer by saying, "Who would like to extend the invitation to the Sanchez family?"

A quick planning activity to end each team discussion might include the questions: **1** What are we going to do? **2** How are we going to do it? **3** Who's going to do what? and **4** When will it be done?

Finalized assignments should be recorded. One way to do this is to keep brief meeting notes that are distributed to all participants after the team meeting.

TIP #6: FOLLOW UP

It is better to not make an assignment than to make one that won't be followed up on. Understandably, leaders are often eager to address the more current needs and sometimes overlook previous commitments. But once a practice of selective follow up is established, team members quickly learn that it isn't necessary to feel accountable for accomplishing assignments. This is a common, but damaging, leadership mistake.

Jesus taught this essential concept of accountability and follow up through parables including one often called "the parable of the wise steward." In this parable, a master gives each of his three servants some resources (money) to watch over during his absence. To one servant he gives five talents, to another he gives two talents, and to the third he gives one. Importantly, when the master returns, he asks for a report on the servants' stewardships. The servants to whom the lord had given the most talents both doubled the master's investment and each received the praise: "Well done, thou good and faithful servant: thou hast been faithful over a few things, I will make thee ruler over many things: enter thou into the joy of thy lord" (Matthew 25: 21, 23). But the third servant feared his master and instead of investing the talent, he dug a hole and buried it so he would not lose it. The lord was displeased: "His lord answered and said unto him, Thou wicked and slothful servant, thou knewest that I reap where I sowed not, and gather where I have not strawed: Thou oughtest therefore to have put my money to the exchangers, and then at my coming I should have received mine own with usury. Take therefore the talent from him, and give it unto him which hath ten talent" (Matthew 25:26–28).

We will discuss this idea of stewardship and accountability in more depth in later chapters, but this parable teaches that leaders should **1** expect much of those they lead, **2** subsequently hold them accountable for obtaining good results, and **3** provide performance feedback. In my experience, substandard performance is more often the fault of the leader than the individual performer. A leader who neglects to provide clear assignments and follow up on them almost always suboptimizes productivity and organizational effectiveness.

The Christlike leader creates a workable method to follow up on all commitments. One simple way to make this method routine is to have the first thing on your team meeting agenda be reports on previous assignments.

TIP #7: SUPPORT TEAM MEMBERS

Leaders can sometimes unintentionally undermine those over whom they have stewardship. This is often a result of leaders wanting to help team members who have come to them directly with their disagreements with other team members who report to that leader.

When possible, it is far better to support the other members of your team(s) and urge those with concerns to try a little harder to resolve their issues directly with the other individual (instead of through you). If a change needs to be made to a decision, work with that team member directly and encourage them to be the one that makes the revision, rather than having it come from you. Don't undermine their authority or allow them not to learn from a mistake by taking things over for them yourself.

One of my graduate school professors was Stephen Covey, the renowned author and leadership guru. He shared a personal experience about how important it is to support those you lead.

He once served as the presiding authority over the missionaries from my church in Ireland, and was concerned about his first meeting with his area supervisor. During the meeting, some of the people who were also in attendance voiced concerns directly to the area supervisor about issues that were part of the new mission president's stewardship. Instead of addressing the issues himself, the supervisor said: "These, of course, are for your mission president's attention. I'm here to sustain and help him. He will deal with these matters."[2]

Had the area supervisor been sympathetic to the views of the people who expressed concerns, or had he started to solve the problems himself, the Irish church leaders would have continued to look to the supervisor for guidance instead of to the young mission president. Instead, Covey reported that he felt sustained by his leader: "How responsible I felt! How committed! How motivated to make things work! How open I was to his teachings of correct principles and help!"[3]

This approach is smart for another reason as well. Once a leader begins to assume the responsibilities of others, he or she will have to continue shouldering the work that should be done by others.

Note that in the previous example about the wise steward, the lord of the servants didn't reassign the failed responsibility of the third servant (the one who was given only one talent and buried it) until "after a long time." I think Christ was teaching that people should be given a reasonable chance to complete their tasks before the leader makes changes. Note also that the resolution of that problem wasn't for the leader to assume the stewardship himself. Instead he transferred the stewardship of the one talent to the servant who had been the wise steward of ten talents.

TIP #8: PRAISE ACCOMPLISHMENTS

Sometimes, the tyranny of the urgent makes us forget to take the time to praise team members for a job well done. This is inconsistent with the actions of a Christlike leader. Just as his disciples all hoped to hear from Christ, "Well done, thou good and faithful servant" (Matthew 25:21), so should we acknowledge the effective service offerings of team members. Your acknowledgements needn't be grand or flowery. Usually an authentic "thank you" will do, but another way to praise the work of team members is to help them understand how their work positively affected key results. You might say something such as, "Lydia, I hope you can see how all of your planning and preparation work for the summer camp has paid off. There's no way we could have pulled off the craft workshops without your help in contacting and training the teachers."

A NOTE ON FAMILY COUNCILS

One of the most important and least discussed teams in the leadership literature is the family. It is a wise family that learns how to adapt the team concept to their unique situation so that everyone can learn how to make good choices and accept responsibility within the safety of the home environment.

SUMMARY

Eight tips for leading teams include: **1** Facilitate, don't dominate, **2** Encourage participation, **3** Don't micromanage, **4** Summarize and clarify, **5** Drive discussions to action, **6** Follow up, **7** Support team members, and **8** Praise accomplishments. A leader who wishes to follow the example of Jesus Christ will consider using these techniques to empower the teams within his or her stewardship.

One of the empowerment tools that isn't mentioned in these eight tips—only because it is so important that it deserves its own chapter—is delegation. In the next chapter we will discuss it in more detail.

NOTES

1.   Muriel Maignan Wilkins, "Signs That You're a Micromanager," *Harvard Business Review*, November 11, 2014, accessed August 17, 2015, https://hbr.org/2014/11/signs-that-youre-a-micromanager.

2.   Stephen R. Covey, "How Do You Get Others to Be Self-Motivated?" *Ensign*, February 1972, accessed February 19, 2015, http://www.lds.org.

3.   Ibid.

Thou wilt surely wear away, both thou, and this people that is with thee: for this thing is too heavy for thee; thou art not able to perform it thyself alone. (Exodus 18:18)

LESSON 6
DELEGATE

After my wife and business partner Mareen and I started our consulting and training firm, I was asked to be a bishop in our church, the Church of Jesus Christ of Latter-day Saints. The LDS Church uses a lay ministry, and the position of bishop is the equivalent of a Priest or Minister of a local congregation—called a ward—with about five hundred members. It is generally a five-year assignment with responsibilities that consume about twenty hours each week. I already had heavy leadership responsibilities and travel commitments with my consulting firm, and although I felt honored to serve in the church, I was overwhelmed. Seeking counsel from a friend who had also been a bishop, I asked him how he had managed to lead a ward while having a busy full-time job at the same time. He declared that I must "delegate or die!"

He wasn't the first to offer that advice. When Moses was bending under the load of his assignment, his father-in-law Jethro advised him similarly:

> And it came to pass on the morrow, that Moses sat to judge the people: and the people stood by Moses from the morning unto the evening. And when Moses' father in law saw all that he did to the people, he said, What is this thing that thou doest to the people? why sittest thou thyself alone, and all the people stand by thee from morning unto even? . . . The thing that thou doest is not good. Thou wilt surely wear away, both thou, and this people that is with thee: for this thing is too heavy for thee; thou art not able to perform it thyself alone. Hearken now unto my voice, I will give thee counsel, and God shall be with

thee: . . . thou shalt provide out of all the people able men . . . and it shall be, that every great matter they shall bring unto thee, but every small matter they shall judge: so shall it be easier for thyself, and they shall bear the burden with thee. (Exodus 18:13–14, 17–19, 21–22)

Sounds like Jethro's version of "Delegate or die!"

FINDING BALANCE

Without delegation, few leaders could be successful. And it is important to not only share the workload of leadership, but to prepare future leaders as well. When one of my church leaders spoke to the Young Presidents Organization (a peer support organization for chief executive officers and senior business leaders), he explained why Christ led in this manner: "Other leaders have sought to be so omnicompetent that they have tried to do everything themselves, which produces little growth in others. Jesus trusts his followers enough to share his work with them so that they can grow. That is one of the greatest lessons of his leadership."[1]

But delegation is not as simple as turning over work to others. That's why many leaders don't do it. It requires planning and coaching, often taking more time in the beginning than if the leader simply does the job by himself or herself. Bill Dyer, one of my BYU professors, explains: "Delegation is not just a gimmick to get rid of work. It is a leadership strategy—a larger plan in which the leader is eventually relieved of certain activities and the person receiving tasks experiences growth and development in the new area of work. Effective delegation is the result of serious planning, a clear explanation of what is involved, proper training, follow-through, and a willingness to let go."[2]

Dyer instructs that leaders can delegate assignments (a single task), projects (a more complex set of tasks), or areas of work (a complex set of activities that persists over time). Depending on what is delegated, the leader must invest increasingly significant amounts of time, energy, and trust. And he warns: "Any good leader knows, however, that delegation won't necessarily give him more free time immediately. In the long run, effective delegation should give the leader more time for other matters, but in the short time frame, it may involve an even greater time commitment."[3]

More recently, Jeffrey Pfeffer, the Thomas D. Dee II Professor of Organizational Behavior at Stanford University's Graduate School of

Business, explained that the reason many managers don't delegate is because they think it takes too much effort. Others feel that subordinates won't do the delegated work as well as the manager does. But this short-term focus—what Pfeffer calls "the self-enhancement bias"—can be detrimental to both the leader and the organization. Results are suboptimized and the leader becomes irreplaceable.[4] No leader can afford to see himself or herself as irreplaceable. Even Jesus Christ, arguably the best leader in history, knew that for the good of his organization and its future leaders he had to delegate.

HOW CHRIST DELEGATED

Jesus Christ was a master of delegation and personal development. Let's consider seven of his leadership practices in this regard that are recorded in the four gospels of the New Testament (see figure 6-1).

KEY DELEGATION PRACTICES:

1. Use organizational structure
2. Transfer specific authority
3. Give significant responsibility, not just minor tasks
4. Be clear about the responsibility and its importance
5. Demonstrate confidence that the person can accomplish the responsibility
6. Create a "return and report" accountability system
7. Avoid reassuming the delegated responsibility

Figure 6-1: Six Practices for Effective Delegation

1. USE ORGANIZATIONAL STRUCTURE

Christ established a church structure that relied on delegated authority by calling twelve apostles and a quorum of seventy whom he commissioned to carry on the work in his name. Of the calling of the twelve, Luke writes: "Then he called his twelve disciples together, and gave them power and authority over all devils, and to cure diseases. And he sent them to preach the kingdom of God, and to heal the sick" (Luke 9:1–2). And of the seventy he reports: "After these things the Lord appointed other seventy also, and sent them two and two before his face into every city and place, whither he himself would come" (Luke 10:1). Formal organizational structures allow a mechanism for delegation and leadership development.

2. TRANSFER SPECIFIC AUTHORITY

This account of establishing a structure for delegation also illustrates that effective delegation requires the transfer of specific authority. The delegatee must understand exactly what they have the delegated authority to do (as indicated further in later verses in Luke 10). In the Luke account of the commissioning of apostles, note how Christ gives not just clear assignments (i.e., to preach the kingdom of God) but also the specific authority to do the assignment, which in this case includes, the authority "over all devils" and "to cure diseases." A leader who delegates an assignment without also giving the authority to complete the assignment, has done only part of the job. I have seen on many occasions, for example, the frustration a delegatee has when his or her leader gives the assignment to do something without the power to authorize the relevant decisions or spend budget money to accomplish the assigned task. It is a prescription for failure.

3. GIVE SIGNIFICANT RESPONSIBILITY, NOT JUST MINOR TASKS

When Christ delegated, he gave significant responsibility and was neither paternalistic nor condescending. He instructed Peter, for example, to "strengthen his brethren"—an assignment with broad scope and significance (see Luke 22:32). To the twelve he gave the assignment, "Go ye into all the world, and preach the gospel to every creature" (Mark 16:15) and he delegated power over unclean spirits and the responsibility to heal all manner of sickness and disease (Matthew 10:1).

Peter took his assignments seriously. At the day of Pentecost, three thousand souls were "pricked in their heart" and accepted his invitation to "repent, and be baptized . . . in the name of Jesus Christ" (Acts 2:37–38). Five thousand more had accepted his message only a few days later in Jerusalem (Acts 3:19; Acts 4:4).

This delegated authority culminated in Peter raising a beloved woman from the dead in the way he had observed Christ raise a child: "But Peter put them all forth, and kneeled down, and prayed; and turning him to the body said, Tabitha, arise. And she opened her eyes: and when she saw

Peter, she sat up. And he gave her his hand, and lifted her up, and when he had called the saints and widows, presented her alive" (Acts 9:40–41).

When he healed a lame man, Peter made clear from whence this delegated authority had come: "Why look ye so earnestly on us, as though by our own power or holiness we had made this man to walk? . . . Jesus, whom ye delivered up . . . his name hath made this man strong" (see Acts 3:12–16).

Note that Jesus didn't restrict the autonomy or choice of others by requiring a particular methodology for accomplishing the responsibilities he delegated. Instead, he expected others to figure out their own best method of accomplishing the assignment.

4. BE CLEAR ABOUT THE RESPONSIBILITY AND ITS IMPORTANCE

Christ was clear in delegating responsibility and helping people understand the importance of the delegated task. At the sea of Tiberias, for example, he instructed Peter to "feed my lambs" (John 21:15). To add emphasis and ensure understanding he repeated the instruction twice more, using the slightly different words "feed my sheep" (John 21:16–17). Interestingly, before delegating this responsibility, Christ reminded Peter of why the assignment was so important, and why Peter must motivate himself to accomplish it, by preceding the delegation with the question: "Lovest thou me?" (John 21:15). Thus motivated by the love of his mentor, the same Peter who in his weakness had thrice denied the Christ, eventually became a leader so powerful in his delegated authority that people would line the streets "that at the least the shadow of Peter passing by might overshadow some of them" and heal them (Acts 5:15).

Surely Christ knew that his efforts to teach, develop, and delegate to Peter would be worth it in the end. Can we have less faith in those we are charged to develop, even when they seem unable to accomplish the tasks required?

5. DEMONSTRATE CONFIDENCE THAT THE PERSON CAN ACCOMPLISH THE DELEGATED RESPONSIBILITY

When Jesus instructed Peter to launch out into the deep and cast his net over the side of his boat, Peter had been laboring mightily all night and was certain that there were no fish to be caught. Nevertheless, something about Christ's confident instruction caused him to cast in his net one more time. As you may know, the size of the catch threatened to burst the net and capsize two vessels. But a much bigger test of faith and obedience was yet to come. As Peter reached the shore of Galilee, Christ invited him to leave his profession and accept a delegated assignment as a disciple and future senior leader of Christ's church. Inspired by the confidence Jesus showed in him, Peter abandoned everything—not just his livelihood, but everything that he knew and trusted, his associations, his community, his life. Luke says simply of this life-rocking event that Peter "forsook all, and followed him" (Luke 5:11). Can you imagine what it would take to forsake *everything*?

Although this says much about Peter, it also says something about the way Christ delegated. Even with assignments that seemed life shattering, massive, incomprehensible, or impossible, when Jesus delegated some authority or assignment, he did it in a way that made people think they could accomplish what he expected of them. Can you imagine being in a boat in stormy seas and watching Jesus approaching you, walking on the water? Can you imagine him extending his hand to you and inviting you to join him on the rolling sea? But when he delegated the power to master the elements to Peter, he did it in a way that inspired the brave man to jump overboard, where he briefly "walked on the water, to go to Jesus" (Matthew 14:29).

A Christlike leader would certainly not ask something of a follower that would shatter his or her self-esteem or abilities. We have to assume Christ asked extraordinary things of Peter because he knew that this great leader, with faith and effort, could walk on water, heal the sick, and raise the dead. But to some in our charge, an assignment to speak publically, or run a challenging project, may seem just as impossible to them as walking on water did to Peter. The delegatee should feel that the leader believes that he or she is capable of accomplishing the task. And he or she should be confident that the leader will always be available to offer appropriate assistance.

It is easier to walk on water when you can see your leader floating in front of you, hand outstretched before you.

6. CREATE A "RETURN AND REPORT" ACCOUNTABILITY SYSTEM

Christ held Peter accountable for his shortcomings, lovingly helping him to learn from his mistakes and develop into the superb leader the senior apostle would eventually become. This concept of effective steward-ship is taught in the scriptures and demonstrated by Jesus: "And he called him, and said unto him, How is it that I hear this of thee? give an account of thy stewardship; for thou mayest be no longer steward" (Luke 16:2).

Remember that Christ never punished Peter for his missteps. Peter was hard enough on himself. Can't you feel his regret and disappointment when he "weeps bitterly" at his failures to acknowledge the Lord he loves, or fails to meet his expectations? (see Luke 22:62). But Peter's disappoint-ment is instructional and transformative. The return and report function of delegation serves that purpose. It is never a place for harsh words, but for instruction and support. And when a task is well accomplished, the return and report follow-up discussion is an opportunity for positive acknowledgement and appropriate praise.

I once served with a church leader who had the philosophy that an important part of his role was to "catch people doing something good." I saw the smiles and feelings of accomplishment those within his steward-ship had when at the end of a return and report activity he would say, sometimes with tears of appreciation in his eyes, "Well done. I believe the Lord would be pleased with your work."

7. AVOID REASSUMING THE DELEGATED RESPONSIBILITY

As has been mentioned in a previous chapter, we only see Christ taking back delegated authority for unworthiness, not weak performance. Peter was never removed from the apostleship for his missteps. And we have no record of Christ ever saying, "Never mind, Peter. I'll just do it myself." What would Peter have learned from that?

SUMMARY

Delegation is critical for leaders both because the responsibilities of leadership are so heavy and because great opportunities exist therein to develop future leaders. Jesus Christ is a marvelous exemplar of these lead-ership techniques and demonstrates effective delegation with the apos-tle Peter and others, including how to: **1** Use organizational structure; **2**

Transfer specific authority; **3** Give significant responsibility, not just minor tasks; **4** Be clear about the responsibility and its importance; **5** Demonstrate confidence that the person can accomplish the delegated responsibility; **6** Create a "return and report" accountability system; and **7** Avoid reassuming the delegated responsibility.

In the next chapter let's review an especially challenging leadership mandate: how to resolve conflict.

NOTES

1.   Spencer W. Kimball, "Jesus: The Perfect Leader," *Ensign*, August 1979, accessed January 16, 2015, http://www.lds.org.

2.   William G. Dyer, "Why, How, and How Not to Delegate: Some Hints for Home and Church," *Ensign*, August 1979, accessed February 23, 2015, http://www.lds.org.

3.   Ibid.

4.   Amy Gallo, "Why Aren't You Delegating?" *Harvard Business Review*, July 26, 2012, accessed August 17, 2015, https://hbr.org/2012/07/why-arent-you-delegating&cm.

Blessed are the peacemakers: for they shall be called the children of God. (Matthew 5:9)

LESSON 7
RESOLVE CONFLICTS

When Mareen and I started The Fisher Group, we contacted a number of potential clients to get their recommendations on how we should expand our training portfolio. We were a little surprised to see that the most common request was for training about conflict resolution. "Please help us," they would say, "learn how to overcome disagreements," or "manage personality conflicts," or "stop fights," or "heal rifts in our organization." Further investigation convinced us that some forms of conflict were *inevitable* in the workplace, and that if teams were unable to successfully resolve it, that organizational effectiveness—and sometimes even individual health and safety—would be compromised.

This is not a new problem. The apostle Paul wrote to the Corinthians: "But if any man seem to be contentious, we have no such custom, neither the churches of God. Now in this that I declare unto you I praise you not, that ye come together not for the better, but for the worse. For first of all, when ye come together in the church, I hear that there be divisions among you; and I partly believe it" (1 Corinthians 11:16–18).

The most common use of the words "conflict" and "contention" in the Bible are in conjunction with wars—the armed consequence of the extreme end of the continuum of disagreement. But the term is also used elsewhere to describe more common problems that affect all organizations: personal or organizational disagreements on procedures and practices.

Some of these recorded disputes have to do with status or jealousy. Christ himself had to deal with some of this with his own disciples, as noted in this pithy observation in Luke: "And there was also a strife among

[the twelve apostles], which of them should be accounted the greatest"
(Luke 22:24).

A FEW TIPS ON HOW TO RESOLVE CONFLICT

My professor, Bill Dyer, often taught that the first step of resolving conflict was to understand the cause. His experience indicated that *most* conflict originates from a single thing. Would you like to know what accounts
for most of the conflict that, when unresolved, can ultimately result in
splintered organizations, shattered friendships, and broken homes?

The technical answer is "violated expectations." What that means is
that party A thinks that party B is going to do something, but party B
does something different. Think about it. When was the last time you
felt conflict towards someone else? Chances are that it was because you
thought someone was going to complete an assignment but they didn't—
you expected your son to help you with the dishes but he plopped onto
the couch to play video games instead. You thought your friend was going
to come over and help you move, your spouse was going to pick up your
daughter after school, your team member would be appreciative for something you did for her—but something else happened. That's a violated
expectation. You thought X was going to happen but it didn't. Y happened
instead.

A KEY TO UNDERSTANDING CONFLICT RESOLUTION:

Most conflict is caused by VIOLATED EXPECTATIONS

Figure 7-1: The most Common Cause of Conflict

At this point the conflict is small, and it is usually possible to resolve
it through thoughtful discussion. But without discussion, these situations
often grow into deeper conflict and contention. Sometimes people can
become offended and even destroy relationships as a result of what almost
always starts as a small disappointment.

TIPS FOR RESOLVING CONFLICT:

1. Discuss expectations *early*
2. Find some common ground to build on

Figure 7-2: Tips for Conflict Resolution

DISCUSS EXPECTATIONS

If the violated expectation isn't discussed and resolved early, normal feelings of confusion or disappointment or embarrassment often turn into secondary emotions such as resentment or anger. Once a secondary emotion is attached, the conflict starts a sort of pressurized fire inside us, and resolution becomes increasingly difficult. Ironically, attempts to avoid the conflict by ignoring it or staying silent during these early stages, may actually deepen the problem as the unresolved anger expands like lava bubbling inside of a volcano waiting until its poisonous gas can no longer be contained. This is especially true if similar unresolved situations have occurred previously. The situations accumulate; building more and more pressure that requires some sort of venting to resolve safely. If the anger continues to build until it erupts uncontrollably, it causes compounding damage. If the eruption occurs internally, serious emotional or spiritual destruction occurs. If the eruption is external, hurtful words may be spewed that, upon reflection, the individual later wishes they could retract. People in the path of the eruption can be seriously burned even if they had nothing to do with the original problem. The dark steam of contention covers those affected like a thick blinding cloud of ash.

Instead, you might say something soon after the violated expectation occurs, such as: "Weston, was I mistaken in assuming that you were going to notify Brandon that the project was two weeks behind schedule? He called me and said he felt blindsided," or "Son, didn't we agree that we'd do the dishes together? I feel sad when I am left to do them without you after I worked so hard to make dinner in the first place," or "Gage, did we have a miscommunication about our move? I felt a little let down when you didn't come over to help," or "Sweetheart, did I get mixed up about who was picking up Hanna? I thought we agreed you were going to do it," or "Kenzie, I felt a little disappointed that you never mentioned that I covered your shift for you last Wednesday. You're usually so appreciative."

Once the expectation is expressed, several things can happen. First, you might find that your expectation was never communicated properly. It is not fair to hold someone else accountable for anything they did not know you expected of them. "Sorry, honey, I didn't know I was supposed to pick up Hanna." Second, you might discover that your expectation was understood differently than you intended. "Oops. I thought the move was next Thursday, not last Thursday. I feel really bad about that." Third, you may come to understand that your expectation was communicated and understood, but not agreed to. "I thought you understood that I would take a shift for you later. Isn't that thanks enough?" Fourth, you may come to understand that there are reasons for the expectation not being met. "I totally forgot about calling Brandon. I'm sorry." Or fifth, you might find that the expectation was understood but that the other party decided not to do what was expected of them. "I don't want to do the dishes."

To follow Christ's leadership example, you will learn from the first two instances to be more effective in setting and communicating expectations. From the third you will learn that expectations need to be realistic and agreed to in order to be effective. From the fourth you'll learn compassion and patience. And from the fifth you will learn how to teach, correct, and forgive. Your positive personal experiences dealing with conflict situations will enable you to help others with them as well.

FIND COMMON GROUND

In our professional responsibilities we have been called on to help resolve deep-seated conflict between labor and management, organizational functions, or powerful feuding managers. Honestly, in these types of deep, long lasting conflict, there is nothing we know of that can guarantee a successful resolution of the conflict every time. Sometimes talking about violated expectations helps, and sometimes it is too late for that. But those times we have seen an effective resolution, the people have been able to agree on some type of common ground: a shared objective that superseded their differences and allowed them to do the difficult and often humbling work of reconciliation. So too, we must find a reason to help those suffering from conflict to rise above their differences in order to heal our organizations, communities, and homes.

A wise leader helps those struggling with conflict to find that shared objective. For example, as a bishop I had many discussions with couples in peril. I would often ask: "What is a goal you can both agree to work toward?" Some would say: "To save our marriage," others "To do whatever we can to help our children," or "To eliminate contention and restore the harmony in our home." Those that could find a mutually agreeable goal were often successful in the difficult tasks of resolving their differences. Those that couldn't agree on a shared goal were seldom able to make any meaningful progress.

Another one of my BYU professors, Bonner Ritchie, participated in conflict resolution discussions between the leaders of the Arabs and the Jews in Palestine. In even one of the most intractable conflicts of all history, he reported that they were able to find one area of common ground that allowed them to make advancements to resolve a few significant disagreements: they each wanted their children to have peace some day.

George Mitchell, who served as the majority leader of the Democratic Party in the U.S. Senate from 1980 to 1995, speaks of another seemingly intractable conflict. When he met with the then leader of the Republican Party—Bob Dole—to try to create an agreement that would foster bipartisan cooperation in the management of the Senate, he and Dole quickly agreed to the common ground objective of working together to serve the best interests of the United States. But with such deeply conflicting views about what those best interests were and how to serve them, he also suggested a mutual agreement as to *how* they might work together. Mitchell promised to **1** "never surprise him," **2** "give him as much notice as possible of every action I intended to take," **3** "never criticize him personally or try to embarrass him," **4** "always be available to him," and **5** "always keep my word" whenever it was humanly possible.[1] Dole agreed. The result was a unique spirit of cooperation that has been difficult to replicate since that time.

After serving in the Senate, Mitchell—not surprisingly—went on to become a prominent peace negotiator. At one point, he was the U.S. envoy to Northern Ireland and was instrumental in resolving the armed conflict between the Protestants and Catholics famously known as "the troubles." He believes that all successful conflict resolution must include three things: **1** "knowledge about the history and nature of the conflict"; **2** "a recognition that the people involved must own the resolution," meaning that they must literally create the agreement themselves using their own words; and **3** "deep reservoirs of patience and perseverance."[2]

HOW CHRIST RESOLVED CONFLICT

A remarkable illustration of how to resolve conflict can be found after Jesus concluded praying in the Garden of Gethsemane. Imagine what it must have been like to stand in the garden when "a great multitude with swords and staves, from the chief priests and the scribes and the elders" (Mark 14:43) came to capture and imprison Jesus for capital crimes he had never committed. As Judas approached: "Jesus said unto him, Friend, wherefore art thou come? Then came they, and laid hands on Jesus, and took him" (Matthew 26:50).

Notice here, how Christ attempts to diffuse the situation by using words such as "friend," despite the fact that he spoke to a betrayer. His confronters outnumbered his followers, the mob clearly had evil designs, and they carried weapons. I have to assume with these wording choices that Jesus also used a calm and comforting tone of voice, even though the multitude probably assaulted ("laid hands on") him (Matthew 26:50).

The affront on Christ was too much for Peter who, in the heat of the conflict, flashed his sword and severed the right ear of Malchus, the servant of the high priest (See John 18:7–12): "And Jesus answered and said, Suffer ye thus far. And he touched his ear, and healed him" (Luke 22:51).

I wonder how many of us would display compassion for someone who was threatening our life? The Garden healing is a remarkable example of forgiveness and charity—the true love of Christ. How many conflicts could be resolved if each party thought less about their own pain and more about the wounds of their enemy?

Matthew's account then adds this kind but firm rebuke of Peter: "Then said Jesus unto him, Put up again thy sword into his place: for all they that take the sword shall perish with the sword" (Matthew 26:52), suggesting that confronting violence with violence is not his approved method of dealing with conflict.

How did Christ resolve the conflict once it had escalated to physical violence? Did he fight back? No, he healed the ear of one of his attackers. He displayed compassion rather than anger, self-control rather than rage. But he still bravely stood his ground, asking those who attacked him why they hadn't tried to capture him earlier in a public setting, probably pricking their hearts for the cowardly method of approaching him virtually unprotected, under the cloaking cover of darkness (Luke 22:52–53). Jesus, ever the master teacher of morality, risked a provocation of his armed oppressors with his response.

He felt he had the power to extricate himself, but didn't use it, because this conflict was part of what was required of him by his father. He explained: "Thinkest thou that I cannot now pray to my Father, and he shall presently give me more than twelve legions of angels? But how then shall the scriptures be fulfilled, that thus it must be?" (Matthew 26:53–54).

In John's account we next read: "Jesus answered, I have told you that I am he: if therefore ye seek me, let these go their way: That the saying might be fulfilled, which he spake, Of them which thou gavest me have I lost none" (John 18:8–9).

I include this part of the story to emphasize that Christ negotiated with his captors to free his friends because he wanted the disciples to be safe. I have counseled people who thought it was necessary for them to remain, for example, in physically or emotionally abusive situations, convincing themselves somehow that the Christlike thing to do in the midst of their conflict was to endure further unnecessary suffering as a way to "turn the other cheek" or display forgiveness for their tormentors. I believe this example from the last days of Jesus's life demonstrates that he did not expect people to do anything of that sort. Instead, Christ expects his followers to be safe and to protect themselves (and those depending on them) from avoidable harm. When Christ said, "whosoever shall smite thee on thy right cheek, turn to him the other also," (Matthew 5:39) I believe that he was encouraging courage and patience, not self-destructiveness. As this scripture in the Garden indicates, he values our safety and well-being. We should value it, too.

CONFLICT-RESOLUTION METHODS DISPLAYED BY THE SAVIOR

From this account, we can extrapolate the following tips for resolving conflict situations as Jesus Christ would:

SIX WAYS CHRIST RESOLVED CONFLICT:

1. Remain calm. In conflict situations use soothing words and a calming tone.
2. Don't lower yourself to the tactics of others. Christ didn't call down avenging angels even though he was unjustly attacked and accused. He didn't fight back with the weapons used against him, either, even though those around him had weapons and felt it was a justifiable response.
3. Don't escalate the conflict. Although it is difficult to not lash out when we are angry, Christ's approach was to display patience, long-suffering, and personal control. He tried to diffuse the situation rather than escalate it.

4. Strive to heal those with whom you are in conflict. Demonstrate compassion and sympathy for their pain. Anybody can love their friends, but Christ taught to love our enemies: "But I say unto you, Love your enemies, bless them that curse you, do good to them that hate you, and pray for them which despitefully use you, and persecute you" (Matthew 5:44).

5. Stand up for yourself bravely in a firm and loving manner, but

6. Don't place anyone in harm's way.

Figure 7-3: Christ's Approach to Conflict Resolution

SUMMARY

Although it is unlikely that we will ever achieve a complete elimination of conflict and contention, there is much we can do to reduce it, at least within the areas of our stewardships as leaders. Understanding that conflict is often caused by violated expectations and can be reduced by openly and honestly discussing these violations as soon after they occur as possible is a key insight. And finding common ground is also useful, especially a shared goal that is equally desirable to both parties in conflict, allowing them to rise above their individual concerns and do the difficult work of reconciliation.

The capture of Christ in the Garden of Gethsemane offers additional insight into how Christlike leaders can deal with difficult conflict situations: **1** Remain calm. **2** Don't lower yourself to the tactics of others. **3** Don't escalate the conflict. **4** Strive to heal those with whom you are in conflict. **5** Stand up for yourself bravely in a firm and loving manner, but **6** Don't place anyone in harms way.

In the next chapter we will deal with a leadership temptation that faces almost every leader, and has destroyed many: How to avoid "unrighteous" dominion.

NOTES

1. Alison Beard, "Life's Work: An Interview with George Mitchell," *Harvard Business Review*, June 2015, accessed August 17, 2015, http://hbr.org/2015/06/george-mitchell.

2. Ibid.

To him be glory and dominion for ever and ever. Amen.
(1 Peter 5:11)

LESSON 8
AVOID UNRIGHTEOUS DOMINION

Before Mareen and I started our consulting firm, we worked in human resources assignments with Procter & Gamble, Tektronix, and Weyerhaeuser. We sometimes heard complaints from employees about a leader who had said or done something wrong. These reports were especially troubling when they involved actions that were dominating, controlling, or even emotionally abusive. The effects of these leadership errors were significant, often reducing morale, slashing productivity, and decimating trust across large swaths of the afflicted organization.

A COMMON LEADERSHIP MISTAKE

Dominion is a word normally used negatively throughout the Bible as a synonym for controlling power and authority, as in Isaiah's acknowledgement that "other lords beside thee have had dominion over us" (Isaiah 26:13). This is the use of the word referred to in chapter two where I contrasted dominion with Christ's model of servant leadership. But as the scripture that opens this chapter suggests, there can be either bad dominion (as exercised by autocratic leaders) or good dominion (as exercised by servant leaders). Leadership power (dominion) is like electricity. It can either generate the energy necessary to enable and amplify the most significant of human accomplishments or it can be the source of scorching and corrupting devastation.

Leaders can exercise dominion either "righteously" or "unrighteously." A Christlike leader assiduously avoids the temptation to unrighteous dominion, but in a world where that type of leadership is common, he or she must take protective steps to avoid the powerful pull of becoming like many other leaders. The widespread abuse of power is so prevalent—both in past and current eras—that virtually everyone has witnessed the consequences of the now trite but still true observation made in 1887 by the historian Lord Acton: "Power tends to corrupt and absolute power corrupts absolutely."[1]

Several years ago, a well-known Fortune 100 company hired my consulting firm to help them create a more empowering, team-based work culture. As part of the effort we conducted an employee survey about leadership, and I became troubled by the opinions we collected about one of the corporate executives. As near as I can remember it, this is the conversation I had with him (I will call him Robert) in his well-appointed corner office where we discussed the feedback:

ME: "Robert, there is an unusually strong perception among the people that report to you that you value hierarchy more than getting improved business results."

ROBERT: "That's because I do."

ME: "Really? So if one of your reports came up with an idea that you believed could improve quality or cut cost, you wouldn't allow it just because it was their idea instead of yours?"

ROBERT (leaning forward): "That's right. I'm sitting in this office and they're not. I fought long and hard to get here. I plan to keep it. No way I'm letting a subordinate show me up. After I retire, and one of them gets promoted, they can do whatever they want."

I remember feeling a begrudging respect for Robert's honesty because normally when I've confronted leaders about these types of problems they are too political to admit that they don't always use their power (of authorization, or funding, or encouragement, and so on) to better the organization they are supposed to be leading. But I have witnessed many leadership behaviors like those displayed by Robert. Too many to count. That's a problem. Because technically, using the powers of office for anything other than the reasons for which they are intended is an abuse of those powers. It is unrighteous dominion.

ABUSE OF POWER

Let's drill down into an example that is more troubling. I've often wondered how a handful of financial executives could have rationalized the decisions to encourage the authorization and trading of sub-prime housing loans in a way that would result in the plunging of the global economy into the deepest financial woes since the Great Depression. These leaders were savvy and capable, and I reject both the notion that they couldn't foresee the potential consequences of their actions, as well as the argument that their only motivation was greed.

Of course money was a factor, but I believe that for these very rich corporate leaders, the actual wealth became less important than having the *power* to generate it at will. I believe their relentless pursuit for the power to manipulate markets to their advantage had so corrupted them over time that their moral compasses lost the ability to find true north. You can make an argument that the maxim "money is the root of all evil" is wrong. I believe that power holds that dubious distinction. And many have chosen to sacrifice any sort of morality to obtain it.

A few of the sub-prime finance execs paid for what they did, starting the game of dominoes that led to thousands of people losing their homes, tens of thousands losing their jobs, and millions losing about half of their retirement savings—like my wife and I did. But most of those who abused their power to destroy the economy kept their power. And I'm willing to bet that even if you're angry with that, you're not surprised.

MACHIAVELLIAN JUSTIFICATION

The advice Niccolò Machiavelli—arguably the first professional leadership consultant—gave to those who aspire to supreme power is to practice unrighteous dominion. Many still follow his advice today: "Every one admits how praiseworthy it is in a prince to keep faith, and to live with integrity and not with craft. Nevertheless our experience has been that those princes who have done great things have held good faith of little account, and have known how to circumvent the intellect of men by craft, and in the end have overcome those who have relied on their word."[2]

Among those taking Machiavelli's advice are people like Stalin, Hitler, and Pol Pot, who, once having obtained the power they sought, secured and abused their power with an unprincipled vigor. History is full of this social cancer. Richard Nixon lost the presidency of the United States because his spies stole secrets from the Democratic National Committee meeting at the Watergate Hotel. Kim Jong-il, the "Dear Leader" of North Korea, dispatched military commandos to kidnap women and force them to be temporary "concubines."[3] He is believed to have fathered at least nine children with these unwilling "mistresses." Ancient royalty committed patricide and matricide to obtain and preserve their power. Some even killed their own children. At the root of this abuse is the belief that those with the power to make the laws, don't have to live by them.

Obviously these abuses aren't limited to the political arena. Remember Dennis Kozlowski? Tyco's former CEO is currently serving up to twenty-five years in prison for defrauding Tyco's investors. His most famous abuse of power was called the "Tyco Roman Orgy."[4] In 2001, he had his company pay half of a two million dollar birthday party for his second wife. The party on an exclusive Italian island was billed as a shareholder meeting and featured such extravagances as an ice sculpture of David urinating Stolichnaya vodka.

Unrighteous dominion is not consistent with the leadership example of Jesus Christ. It subverts the empowerment of others. It creates disease in the soul.

WHAT CAUSES UNRIGHTEOUS DOMINION?

In our executive coaching work with business and government leaders, we often uncover that the reason they try to dominate or control others comes from a belief that they are superior to those they lead and are therefore above the law. Shockingly, this can even happen in churches, regardless of how clearly inconsistent this assumption is with Christ's teachings. Renowned Christian author C.S. Lewis warns:

> It is a serious thing to live in a society of possible gods and goddesses, to remember that the dullest and most uninteresting person you can talk to may one day be a creature which, if you saw it now, you would be strongly tempted to worship. . . . It is with the awe and the circumspection proper to them, that we should conduct all our dealings with one another, all friendships, all loves, all play, all politics. There are no ordinary people. You have never talked to a mere mortal. Nations, cultures, arts, civilizations—these are mortal, and their life is to ours as the life of a gnat. But it is immortals whom we joke with, work with, marry, snub, and exploit—immortal horrors or everlasting splendors. . . . Next to the Blessed Sacrament itself, your neighbour is the holiest object presented to your senses.[5]

How negative can unrighteous dominion be for a values-based institution? Consider the example of Roger Vangheluwe, the Bishop of Bruges. When he finally admitted to sexually abusing two of his nephews, starting from the time one of the boys was five years old, faithful Catholics were devastated—a violation of trust made worse by the fact that he wasn't prosecuted for the crime because the statute of limitations had expired.[6] In a more recent example, Pope Francis received more than a half of a million signatures on a petition to remove Bishop Robert Finn of Kansas City after his conviction for not reporting suspicion of child abuse among clerics he supervised.[7]

A PERSONAL ASSESSMENT

In our work, Mareen and I are often asked to provide methods that help leaders assess their effectiveness. The best way to do this, of course, is to ask those being led about what they think is working or not working relative to the leader's actions. But another useful tool is what we call a "self-assessment." In that spirit, honestly consider the following questions to determine how much you use the principles of righteousness demonstrated in the New Testament writings about Jesus Christ, rather than the practices or assumptions associated with unrighteous dominion:

1. Do I place the needs of people over the needs of a project, program, or assignment?
2. Do I treat others as I would want to be treated?
3. Would others describe me as humble?
4. Do I respect the views of others, even if I disagree with them?
5. Do people leave interactions with me feeling loved?
6. Do I make requests or do I give orders?
7. Would people say I respect them?
8. Do I ever take credit for others' ideas?
9. Do I accept accountability for my mistakes?
10. Do I blame others when things go poorly?
11. Would others say I'm polite?
12. Would others say I'm supportive and encouraging?
13. Do I ever (even subtly) try to force people to do things?
14. Do I offer assistance more than direction?
15. Would people say that I'm a good listener?

16. While others are speaking, am I thinking of other things, or really listening?
17. Would people say I try to manipulate them?
18. Do I build on other's ideas and suggestions?
19. Do I say things that might be viewed as critical?
20. Do I show appreciation for others? How? Do they feel appreciated?
21. Do I ever withhold approval or love?
22. Do I look for the best in people?
23. Do I ever assume that people have bad intentions?
24. Do I ever think I'm more important than others?
25. Do I ever think that the laws (policies, practices, ethics, standards, and so on) apply differently to me than they do to others?

UNRIGHTEOUS DOMINION	RIGHTEOUS DOMINION
• Power benefits the leader	• Power benefits the organization
• Coercion	• Persuasion
• Impatience	• Long-suffering
• Arrogance	• Gentleness and meekness
• Manipulation	• Love unfeigned
• Cruelty	• Kindness
• Deceit	• Pure knowledge
• Duplicity	• Without hypocrisy
• Cunning	• Without guile

Figure 8-1: The principles of unrighteous versus righteous dominion

HOW CHRIST USED PRINCIPLES OF RIGHTEOUSNESS

Jesus Christ provided an example of righteous leadership. Consider how he dealt with the traitor Judas. Do we hear him chastise him? Withdraw his love? And even though he knew Judas's evil intentions, does he try to coerce him to change his plans? Try to trick him? The answer to all of these questions is no. Instead we see persuasion, long-suffering, gentleness and meekness, love unfeigned, kindness and pure knowledge without hypocrisy or guile.

At the end of the feast of the Passover, Jesus knew that Judas Iscariot—one of his chosen apostles and closest friends—would betray him and cause his death. Christ then remarkably washed the feet of the apostles—even those of Judas—as a sign of his deep and unfeigned love for them (John 13:1–5). A lesser man could not have done that. And one who practices unrighteous dominion would surely not have demonstrated love for his own murderer. At the least he would have tried to dissuade him, with force if necessary, from his cruel intention. Many could have justified much worse in the name of self-defense.

After Peter objected to what he sees as an inappropriate debasing act for the man he believed was the literal Son of God, Jesus addressed Peter's concerns about a master washing the feet of his servants. He then revealed Judas's betrayal. But he did it in a way that the apostles didn't even know whom he was speaking about. There was obviously no pointing of fingers, no raising of the voice, no completely understandable recriminations or reproaches for this most despicable and cowardly plan:

> When Jesus had thus said, he was troubled in spirit, and testified, and said, Verily, verily, I say unto you, that one of you shall betray me. Then the disciples looked one on another, doubting of whom he spake. Now there was leaning on Jesus' bosom one of his disciples, whom Jesus loved. Simon Peter therefore beckoned to him, that he should ask who it should be of whom he spake. He then lying on Jesus' breast saith unto him, Lord, who is it? (John 13:21–25)

And even when Jesus declared who shall betray him, he did it without any attempt to embarrass Judas or sway him from exercising his choices:

> Jesus answered, He it is, to whom I shall give a sop, when I have dipped it. And when he had dipped the sop, he gave it to Judas Iscariot, the son of Simon. And after the sop Satan entered into him. Then said Jesus unto him, That thou doest, do quickly. Now no man at the table knew for what intent he spake this unto him. For some of them thought, because Judas had the bag, that Jesus had said unto him, Buy those things that we have need of against the feast; or, that he should give something to the poor. (John 13:26–29)

Remarkably Christ then gave them a new commandment. Was the commandment that Judas should be stopped? Or that the death of Christ should be revenged? No. Although Christ knew that the betrayal of Judas would cause him to suffer crucifixion—the most painful and hideous death the Romans could devise as a means of discouraging others from even considering rebellion or breaching oppressive laws—Christ commanded that they each love one another. And he didn't exclude Judas from the list of those who should be loved: "A new commandment I give unto you, That ye love one another; as I have loved you, that ye also love one another. By this shall all men know that ye are my disciples, if ye have love one to another" (John 13:34–35).

The account of this incident in Matthew is slightly different, adding a brief interaction between Jesus and his betrayer. But even in this account we see no angry Christ, no justifiably upset leader who forces Judas to change his plan—to have Christ tortured and killed for money. All Jesus did was attempt to dissuade Judas by quoting a scriptural reference, likely with far more concern for the soul of the murderer than for the prevention of his own excruciating suffering: "And as they did eat, he said, Verily I say unto you, that one of you shall betray me. And they were exceeding sorrowful, and began every one of them to say unto him, Lord, is it I? And he answered and said, He that dippeth his hand with me in the dish, the same shall betray me. The Son of man goeth as it is written of him: but woe unto that man by whom the Son of man is betrayed! it had been good for that man if he had not been born. Then Judas, which betrayed him, answered and said, Master, is it I? He said unto him, Thou hast said" (Matthew 26:21–25).

Even later, when the actual betrayal occurs, we see no attempt at unrighteous dominion. Remember that the disciples with Christ had some swords, and were ready to fight to protect themselves. But Jesus commanded them to stand down. I imagine in this next scene, Christ whispering lovingly to the betrayer: "And while he yet spake, behold a multitude, and he that was called Judas, one of the twelve, went before them, and drew near unto Jesus to kiss him. But Jesus said unto him, Judas, betrayest thou the Son of man with a kiss?" (Luke 22:47–48). This is the only recrimination. What remarkable restraint and unfeigned love.

SUMMARY

A Christlike leader avoids unrighteous dominion of any kind and repents when he or she recognizes performing such an act. Unrighteous dominion is widespread, but the Christlike leader would never justify exercising the power granted by his or her organization for any other reason than to benefit the organization. Even if "everyone else is doing it."

In the next chapter we will review what we can learn from Jesus Christ as a master teacher.

NOTES

1.   Lord Acton, in a letter to Bishop Creighton, dated April 3, 1887; cited from David Mathew, *Acton: The Formative Years* (London: Eyre & Spottiswoode, 1946), 185.

2.   Niccolò Machiavelli, *The Prince*, accessed July 17, 2015, http://constitution.org /mac/prince18.htm.

3.   Frances Romero, "Kim Jong Il's Concubines," *Time Magazine*, May 11, 2011, accessed July 18, 2015, http://content.time.com/.../packages/article/0,28804,2071839 _2071844_2071774,00.html.

4.   "Dennis Kozlowski and the Tyco Roman Orgy," *Time Magazine*, May 17, 2011, accessed July 18, 2015, http://content.time.com/time/specials/packages /article/0,28804,2071839_2071844_2071849,00.html.

5.   C.S. Lewis, *The Weight of Glory* (New York: Collier Books, Macmillan Publishing Co., 1980), 18–19.

6.   Steven Erlanger, "Belgian Catholics Remain Anguished by Abuse," *New York Times*, September 19, 2010, accessed July 18, 2015, www.nytimes.com/2010/09/20 /world/europe/20belgium.html.

7.   Philip Pullella, "U.S. Catholic bishop in child pornography case resigns," Reuters, April 21, 2015, accessed July 18, 2015, www.reuters.com/.../2015/04/21/us-pope -abuse-bishop-u-s-idUSKBN0NC15820150421.

And when he was come into his own country, he taught them in their synagogue, insomuch that they were astonished, and said, Whence hath this man this wisdom, and these mighty works? (Matthew 13:54)

LESSON 9
BE A TEACHER

After many years training managers how to be more effective leaders, Mareen and I began to better understand the process of teaching. We noticed, for example, that using stories and examples improved the training. The managers would remember the stories and use them to understand how to apply the instruction to their own situation. We also found that learner-oriented training far surpassed the effectiveness of trainer-oriented workshops. Trainers, for example, who simply lectured from the trainer manuals we provided them, may have covered the required material, but they consistently received much lower scores in teaching effectiveness than those who facilitated active discussions and asked lots of questions to make students think. The use of the case study method, and numerous interactive activities, made workshops more interesting and valuable according to student assessments completed after the training. Sessions where managers shared their ideas and "best practices" with each other were better than those without these practical discussions. Of course this shouldn't have surprised us, since, more than two thousand years ago, Christ—the master teacher—employed all of these techniques.

LEADERS MUST BE TEACHERS

All leaders are teachers. How else can others in their charge develop and improve? In our own leadership development practice, our experience is that these types of coaching activities constitute an increasing percentage of an effective leader's time. Our research indicates, for example, that less effective leaders spend only about ten percent of their time teaching others. However, the most effective leaders spend nearly sixty percent of their time in coaching activities.[1]

Let's examine in more detail some of the teaching methods Christ used that caused the reaction noted in the scripture that opens this chapter. Specifically let's review the use of parables, scriptures, questions, and invitations to act.

FOUR CHRISTLIKE TEACHING TECHNIQUES:

1. Use stories and examples to clarify instruction
2. Base teaching on the accepted canon of your discipline
3. Use questions to engage learners
4. Invite people to act in order to apply and strengthen learning

Figure 9-1: Christ's Teaching Methods

PARABLES

In Mark we read: "And he taught them many things by parables" (Mark 4:2). Matthew adds: "All these things spake Jesus unto the multitude in parables; and without a parable spake he not unto them: That it might be fulfilled which was spoken by the prophet, saying, I will open my mouth in parables; I will utter things which have been kept secret from the foundation of the world" (Matthew 13:34–35).

We know that there are several reasons Christ used this technique of telling a story to illustrate a principle. The curious disciples inquired:

> Why speakest thou unto them in parables? He answered and said unto them, Because it is given unto you to know the mysteries of the kingdom of heaven, but to them it is not given. For whosoever hath, to him shall be given, and he shall have more abundance: but whosoever hath not, from him shall be taken away even that he hath. Therefore speak I to them in parables: because they seeing see not; and hearing they hear not, neither do they understand. (Matthew 13:10–13)

Thus, one reason Jesus used parables was to allow the believers to understand the deeper truth embedded in the teaching while the unbeliever would simply be entertained and unable to understand the true meaning of the revolutionary doctrine Jesus taught. Everybody likes a good story. But Christ acknowledged that this reason was only temporary: "These things have I spoken unto you in proverbs: but the time cometh, when I shall no more speak unto you in proverbs, but I shall shew you plainly of the Father" (John 16:25).

So why else would he use stories? The genius of parables is multi-dimensional. For example, one of my professors in graduate school, Alan Wilkins, researched the topic of how storytelling affects corporate culture for his doctoral thesis at Stanford University.[2] His work indicated that stories are the most powerful way to teach organizational values. Why? Because they help explain complex and important concepts. People can relate them by memory. They spread widely and quickly throughout the organization.

DIFFERENT TYPES OF PARABLES

Stories, comparisons (such as similes and metaphors), and examples are all different types of parables. Christ used them all. We've already discussed stories, but consider this skillful example of using two similes to illustrate and clarify his teachings: "Then said he, Unto what is the kingdom of God like? and whereunto shall I resemble it? It is like a grain of mustard seed, which a man took, and cast into his garden; and it grew, and waxed a great tree; and the fowls of the air lodged in the branches of it. And again he said, Whereunto shall I liken the kingdom of God? It is like leaven, which a woman took and hid in three measures of meal, till the whole was leavened" (Luke 13:18–21).

FOURS WAYS TO ILLUSTRATE TEACHINGS:

1. Detailed and memorable stories
   "I'm reminded of a story of why setting goals is so important. In late 2015, President Obama met with . . ."
2. Similes ("is like" comparison)
3. Metaphors (something different but illuminating)
   "Goals are the indicators on the dashboard of our organization . . ."
4. Examples
   "Let me give you an example of the goals set last year by our senior leadership team to illustrate the wording we might want to use . . ."

Figure 9-2: Types of Parables

As you remember from your high school English classes, a simile compares one thing to another directly by using words such as "like" or "as." A metaphor is another way to compare two things, but this technique omits the words "like" or "as." It declares that the one thing *is* another. Consider this example, which is also about the kingdom of God: "And the scribes which came down from Jerusalem said, He hath Beelzebub, and by the prince of the devils casteth he out devils. And he called them unto him, and said unto them in parables, How can Satan cast out Satan? And if a kingdom be divided against itself, that kingdom cannot stand. And if a house be divided against itself, that house cannot stand" (Mark 3:22–25).

Christ also used examples. For instance, when he taught the apostles how to pray, he certainly wasn't instructing them to only use the prayer we now refer to as The Lord's Prayer (Matthew 6:9–13). But as the master teacher he wanted to give them a specific example of what a prayer might look like, in the same way complex business topics are taught at the Harvard Business School through the case study method.

SCRIPTURES

We have already mentioned how Jesus Christ (as a gospel scholar) used scripture. Obviously a church leader would do the same thing. But leadership outside of religious organizations also demands referencing the appropriate underpinning canons of that institution or discipline. How can one teach physics, for example, without referencing the theories of Einstein, or art without seeing the work of Michelangelo? The best institutional leaders we work with often reference the guiding documents of their operations, be they the charters, mission statements, or constitutions which declare the clear and compelling reason for their existence and the foundational values which cannot be compromised in their organization regardless of circumstance.

QUESTIONS

In his teaching, Christ would often follow a parable with a question. Why did he do that? (Notice that when I ask you a question you stop to think, become more engaged, and pay more attention than you otherwise would.) Asking questions involves the listeners. It doesn't allow them to daydream or be passive or bored. It motivates them to learn.

For example, to answer the question a lawyer had asked of him (who is my brother?), Jesus relayed the parable of the Good Samaritan. After the story he asked the question: "Which now of these three, thinkest thou, was neighbour unto him that fell among the thieves?" The lawyer answered: "He that shewed mercy on him. Then said Jesus unto him, Go, and do thou likewise" (Luke 10:36–37).

Why did Jesus ask that question? Because once the student answered the question, the student knew the lesson of the Good Samaritan. Christ didn't need to repeat it, because the lawyer had already taught himself. And as you know, the lessons we teach ourselves, are much more likely to be remembered and acted upon than those taught to us by another.

In the example above, Christ never stated the lesson. His post-parable questions allow the learners to learn it for themselves.

Note how Christ uses questions to engage the learner in another example: "And, behold, a certain lawyer stood up, and tempted him, saying, Master, what shall I do to inherit eternal life? He said unto him, What is written in the law? how readest thou? And he answering said, Thou shalt love the Lord thy God with all thy heart, and with all thy soul, and with all thy strength, and with all thy mind; and thy neighbour as thyself. And he said unto him, Thou hast answered right: this do, and thou shalt live" (Luke 10:25–28).

By asking skillful questions in these teaching moments, Christ leads the engaged learner to powerful and memorable insights without having to lecture. This allows the learner to apply what they have discovered for themselves instead of what they were told by a teacher.

INVITATIONS TO ACT

At the end of the lesson with the lawyer above, note how Jesus says, "this do, and thou shalt live." This is an invitation to not only hear the teaching but to apply it. Teaching someone something that they will never use is a waste of time. Likewise, the parable of the Good Samaritan illustrates how Jesus invited people to take action. Thus, he says, "Go, and do thou likewise" (Luke 10:37) to the lawyer. And he instructed the woman who was to be stoned for adultery to "go and sin no more," (John 8:11) and the apostles to whom he would teach the Lord's prayer: "After this manner therefore pray ye" (Matthew 6:9).

This teaching method occurs so often in the teachings of Jesus Christ, that I believe a pattern can be suggested. Generally speaking, his teaching method concludes with a call to action. We can emulate this example by asking "will you" questions, such as, "When will you apply this technique we discussed?" or "Will you _____ (accept an assignment, complete a project to apply what we've discussed, put together a plan to implement [something], etc.)?" Engaging in development activities with those you lead is fruitless unless a commitment and a plan to take action are made.

As illustrated by the Christlike method of teaching, people learn best by doing, not just by hearing. I learned a long time ago that teaching someone how to replace the seals in a pump, for example, was never finished until the student had opened a pump and replaced a few seals. Similarly, people learn how to be better public speakers, better leaders, and even how to develop skills such as planning, running effective meetings, creating better organizational structures, and demonstrating empathy, through hands-on practice. To that end, after you read the twelve leadership lessons from the life of Jesus Christ, I encourage you to select projects from the appendix of this book to apply in your own leadership responsibilities. I believe that is the way Christ would have taught these lessons.

SUMMARY

Many regard Jesus Christ as the best teacher of all time. But whether you share that opinion or not, by using the methods he employed, we can improve the effectiveness of the teaching we need to do as leaders. Specifically, by using parables—whether they are stories, similes, metaphors, or examples—we can better clarify instruction and ground it in the practical reality of the learner. We also need, as he did, to use the scriptures of whatever institution or discipline we lead to anchor our teaching to the accepted canon of our organizations. Using questions to engage learners and drive home learning is another powerful technique. And extending an invitation to take action improves the probability that those we teach will be "doers of the word, and not hearers only" (James 1:22).

In the next chapter we will discuss another difficult leadership skill: correcting others.

NOTES

1. The Fisher Group, Inc., "Coach" module handbook, *Leadership Skills Training Program*, 1994–2014.

2. Alan L. Wilkins, *Developing Corporate Character* (San Francisco: Jossey-Bass, 1989), 101–2.

The ear that heareth the reproof of life abideth among the wise. He that refuseth instruction despiseth his own soul: but he that heareth reproof getteth understanding. (Proverbs 5:31–32)

LESSON 10
CORRECT OTHERS PROPERLY

O ne of the most difficult tasks of leadership is the correction of others. I still remember the discomfort I felt as a new manufacturing leader with P&G. Each of the members of my team was older than I was, and I felt odd correcting them.

I don't think I'm alone in this feeling.

Part of the reason so many of us are reluctant to correct others is that we are concerned about hurting feelings or causing offense. But when done properly, correction can, and should, actually be a demonstration of love.

HOW DID JESUS CHRIST CORRECT OTHERS?

Spencer W. Kimball, who served as the president of the LDS Church from 1973 to 1985, illustrated how Christ corrected others:

> Jesus was a patient, pleading, loving leader. When Peter drew his sword and smote the high priest's servant, cutting off his right ear, Jesus said, "Put up thy sword into the sheath" (John 18:11). Without being angry or perturbed, Jesus quietly healed the servant's ear (see Luke 22:51). His reproof of Peter was kind, yet firm.
>
> Because Jesus loved his followers, he was able to level with them, to be candid and forthright with them. He reproved Peter at times because he loved him, and Peter, being a great man, was able to grow from this reproof.[1]

Consider another example from the life of Christ we referenced earlier in the book. Christ demonstrated how to properly correct others in the story of the adulteress. When the Pharisees brought the adulteress to Christ, they demanded to know what he would do with her. She had broken the law and the law dictated that she be stoned for her actions. After drawing in the sand, Jesus responded, "He that is without sin among you, let him first cast a stone at her" (John 8:7). No one picked up a stone. They knew they weren't without sin, "convicted by their own conscience" (John 8:9). One by one the accusers walked away. Finally Jesus "saw none but the woman" and "he said unto her, Woman, where are those thine accusers? hath no man condemned thee? She said, No man, Lord. And Jesus said unto her, Neither do I condemn thee: go, and sin no more" (John 8:10–11).

How much more effective was Christ's reaction towards the woman than if he had given her a lecture, maybe explained the law to her, or even berated her for her bad choices? Instead, we see neither recrimination nor disrespectful language from Christ. There is no evidence of anger. No loss of emotional control. No sarcasm. No chastisement. To the accusers he simply asks them to evaluate their own potential hypocrisy. And, as the scriptures report, they left "being convicted by their own conscience." To the accused he offers calm and loving instruction rather than condemnation. This probably motivated the woman to make changes in her life. Not necessarily because she didn't want to get caught again, but because she wanted to be better.

While this example is instructive for any leader, it is especially helpful for leaders of homes who understand that exhaustion, impatience, and established patterns of behavior can easily interfere with our ability to correct with love. In the home, especially, Christlike leaders cannot allow even stressful corrective situations to devolve into venues for potential abuse or unrighteous dominion. Teresa of Avila—a Roman Catholic saint, Carmelite nun, and reformer of the Carmelite order who lived from 1515 to 1582—explained: "Never when in authority rebuke any one in anger, but only when anger has passed away; and so shall the rebuke bring forth good fruit."[2]

TIPS FOR CORRECTING OTHERS

So how do we correct others properly? Not every incorrect action displayed by those over whom we have stewardship requires leadership reproof. As Pope John XXIII suggested: "See everything. Overlook a great deal. Correct a little."[3]

FIVE SIMPLE TIPS FOR EFFECTIVE CORRECTION:

1. Be certain that the behavior requires correction from you
2. Provide the correction in a timely manner
3. Be clear and precise about what needs to change
4. Ask for a specific improvement
5. Demonstrate genuine caring and support

Figure 10-1: Tips for Correcting Others

Decide whether to intervene by considering the following types of questions:

- What are the probable consequences of not correcting this action/mistake/oversight? Will it cause important damage to anyone? Will our organization suffer if this isn't corrected? Does the importance of the correction outweigh the risk of embarrassment or offense?
- Do I have the information necessary to interject myself into this situation or do I only know part of the story? What do I need to know before I can decide whether to correct or not?
- Am I the right person to offer correction or should it be a different leader?
- Am I sure the situation needs correction, or was someone just doing something differently than I would do it?
- Do I know how to correct the situation or should I get some advice from someone else first? Do I know how to offer loving feedback? If not, is there someone who can help me learn to skillfully do so?
- Is the reason I want to offer correction because of my honest concern for the welfare of the person and our organization, or is it because I want to get something off of my chest?

- Do I have control of my emotions, or will anger, apathy, or resentment make it difficult for me to offer constructive criticism?

If correction is appropriate, it should be delivered as quickly as possible. This is important for both the giver and the receiver of correction. For the receiver, timeliness increases the likelihood that the mistake will be corrected because it is still "fresh." The receiver will likely remember what they did and why they did it and will avoid repeating the mistake or making it habitual. For the one giving the correction, timely reproof reduces the likelihood that a delay will allow anger, distrust, or resentment to build before a discussion can occur.

BE CLEAR

A correction is not useful if the person doesn't understand precisely what was wrong and exactly how to correct it. For example, saying, "Whitley, you need to be a better team member," is not very helpful. Saying, "Whitley, we need to hear more from you in team meetings. Could you come Friday prepared to give a presentation about the status of your project and let us see how we can help you meet next month's deadlines?" is clearer. In the first example, the person only feels judged and chastised. In the latter, the person understands how to improve.

Specific examples are required when giving constructive criticism, so that people understand both what was incorrect and how to improve. General unfocused observations or expectations are insufficient. Don't say, "London, you aren't responsible." Say, "London you came late to three meetings last week." Don't say, "Practik, you aren't kind enough to people." Say, "Practik, when you just now told your sister that you hated her, it made her cry." Don't say, "Ahmed, you have to be more conscientious." Say, "Ahmed, the team needs to know they can count on you. Last Thursday, when you didn't call your customer on time, Joseph and Sabrina each wasted two hours waiting for you."

After you make the correction, ask for an improvement. Christ didn't hesitate to tell the adulteress to sin no more. A Christlike leader will ask London to be on time, Practik to be kind to his sister, and Ahmed to either make his commitments or to let people know beforehand why he cannot.

SHOW FORTH AFTERWARDS AN INCREASE OF LOVE

Brigham Young was famous for being a tough leader during the Mormon pioneer era. But even he gave this recommendation: "If you are ever called to chasten a person, never chasten beyond the balm you have within you to bind up. . . . When you have the chastening rod in your hands, ask God to give you wisdom to use it, that you may not use it to the destruction of an individual, but to his salvation."[4]

After a correction, the caring leader always offers whatever assistance is necessary to help the individual make an improvement. This is a powerful manifestation of love. I also think it is usually a good idea to quickly review the necessary corrections and ensure clarity by asking for questions. Then express confidence that the individual can make any necessary changes. We are all imperfect, and without these corrections from others who care about us, none of us would be able to reach our full potential.

SUMMARY

Although correcting others can be a difficult part of leadership, it is an important skill for the leader who cares enough about organization results to want to help people improve their lives and service. Christ has given us several examples of how to correct others properly, demonstrating both the compassion and the gentle firmness required.

In the next chapter we review how we can learn effective stewardship from the stories of Jesus Christ.

NOTES

1. Spencer W. Kimball, "Jesus: The Perfect Leader," *Ensign*, August 1979, accessed January 16, 2015, http://www.lds.org.

2. Catholic-Pages.com, "Spiritual Maxims: The Maxims of St. Teresa of Avila," accessed January 16, 2015, http://www.catholic-pages.com/grabbag/maxims.asp.

3. United States Conference of Catholic Bishops blog, "John XXIII and Francis: What They Do, But Also How They Do It," USCCBLOG, October 11, 2013, accessed July 18, 2015, usccbmedia.blogspot.com/2013/10/john-xxiii-and-francis-what-they-do-but.html.

4. Brigham Young, "Varieties of Mind, Etc.," *Journal of Discourses*, vol. 9, no. 22 (London: Latter-Day Saints' Book Depot, 1862) 124–25.

His lord said unto him, Well done, good and faithful servant; thou hast been faithful over a few things, I will make thee ruler over many things: enter thou into the joy of thy lord. (Matthew 25:23)

LESSON 11
BE A GOOD STEWARD

One of the most powerful leadership lessons we learn from the ministry of Jesus Christ is the concept of stewardship. In the parable of the talents, for example, Christ taught that a faithful servant should produce good results within the area of his or her assignment. In this chapter, we'll discuss some key principles about how to be a good steward and about how to help those within your stewardship feel a sense of accountability for producing results.

STEWARDSHIP INTERVIEWS

Leaders can't accomplish much by themselves. So how do we generate good results for the organizations we lead? By helping others feel the same sense of accountability for achieving good results as we do. One of the best ways to do this is to create a culture of stewardship through formal and informal discussions on the topic with both groups and individuals. Many organizations we've worked with, for example, incorporate goal reviews or project status reports into regular team meetings and one-on-one interviews.

Jesus Christ demonstrated a technique for this we'll call "a stewardship report"—or in the words of the New Testament, "an account of thy stewardship" (see Luke 16:2).

There is an interesting story found in Matthew including this sort of interview between Christ and a rich young man:

And, behold, one came and said unto him, Good Master, what good thing shall I do, that I may have eternal life? And he said unto him, Why callest thou me good? there is none good but one, that is, God: but if thou wilt enter into life, keep the commandments. He saith unto him, Which? Jesus said, Thou shalt do no murder, Thou shalt not commit adultery, Thou shalt not steal, Thou shalt not bear false witness, Honour thy father and thy mother: and, Thou shalt love thy neighbour as thyself. The young man saith unto him, All these things have I kept from my youth up: what lack I yet? Jesus said unto him, If thou wilt be perfect, go and sell that thou hast, and give to the poor, and thou shalt have treasure in heaven: and come and follow me. But when the young man heard that saying, he went away sorrowful: for he had great possessions. (Matthew 19:16–22)

Even in this brief interaction, we can learn much about how to conduct effective stewardship interviews. There are several tips I'd like to share—most of which are illustrated in this one brief example.

KEYS TO EFFECTIVE STEWARDSHIP INTERVIEWS:

1. Prepare for the interview. Have facts and examples ready
2. Provide time for interaction
3. Let others do most of the talking
4. Respect personal will
5. Demonstrate your concern and appreciation

Figure 11-1: Tips for Stewardship Interviews

1. PREPARE FOR THE INTERVIEW BEFOREHAND

Although this example doesn't indicate that Jesus specifically prepared for the interview, the way he lived his life was so exemplary that when the young man approached him, Jesus was prepared to quote the commandments from memory. Most of us would require a little study time beforehand. Do we know what we want to accomplish in an interaction with another? Do we have the information (goals, feedback, examples, recommendations, and so on) we need to share?

A senior leader of a major corporation whom I admire once told me that he always has "a walking agenda" in his head for each member of his team, so that he can ask questions, provide guidance and encouragement, and conduct a quick informal stewardship interview with anyone he happens to run into at lunch, in the parking lot, or online. This constant level of preparation helps him take better advantage of every interaction he has with those in his stewardship—whether the interaction is a formal meeting or not.

2. PROVIDE TIME FOR INTERACTION

Interestingly, this interview appears to be driven more by the young man than by Jesus. After Christ's response to the young man's initial question, the young man asks another. Jesus answers, and then the young man asks a third question. According to a search I completed while researching this chapter, the words "Jesus answered" appears in the New Testament thirty-nine times, implying that interviews with Christ often included questions from those speaking with him. Allowing time for questions in this manner makes the interview highly interactive and full of discussion instead of it devolving into a one-way lecture in which the interviewee may quickly lose interest and commitment.

Bill Dyer, regarded by many as one of the fathers of the modern "team movement," (and whom I have quoted widely), suggested that a leader ask appropriate personal questions in these interviews to create this type of personal discussion. Noting that many people shy away from these conversations, he suggests: "One can move into the area of personal concern by saying something like the following: 'I honestly would like to know how you feel about your . . . assignment. If you have any qualms or reservations, I would like to know; and if you have any suggestions for improving things, they would be most welcome.' 'How are things going for you now? Are you having any problems, questions, or difficulties with which I can help?' It may be possible to open up a discussion of something you, the leader, have noticed is bothering the other person."[1]

3. LET THEM DO MOST OF THE TALKING

A work colleague who taught me how to conduct professional interviews once told me that a good interviewer listens *much* more than he or she talks. He suggested that interviewers should take no more than 20 percent of the interview time, leaving 80 percent for the interviewee. This can be a challenge while interviewing some people, especially those who tend to answer virtually any question monosyllabically. It helps to ask open-ended questions to get the discussion going. A parent, for example, might ask: "Sweetheart, what are you worried about?" Then listen. Really listen.

One of our favorite memories with our grandnieces and grandnephews comes from when we used to play what we called "the question game" as we drove in the car to family functions. Here's how the question game works: every person in turn gets to ask a question which everyone else has to answer such as, "what is your favorite dessert/school subject/place for vacation?" If you can't think of a question you can pass your turn to the next person. We spent hours making up questions and getting to know each other better through these interactive interviews. We especially liked it when one of the kids would request we play the game as soon as they jumped into our car. The best interviews are often the ones (as illustrated by Christ's example) started by the interviewee.

4. RESPECT PERSONAL WILL

Even though Jesus could have tried to compel the young man, he didn't. Although we may be tempted to cajole, demean, pressure, or argue, a Christlike leader does not use force or guilt-manipulation of any kind.

As former LDS leader Spencer W. Kimball explains: "Jesus' leadership emphasized the importance of being discerning with regard to others, without seeking to control them. He cared about the freedom of his followers to choose. Even he, in those moments that mattered so much, had to choose voluntarily to go through Gethsemane and to hang on the cross at Calvary. He taught us that there can be no growth without real freedom."[2]

5. SHOW LOVE

Perhaps the best way we can demonstrate our confidence in the interviewee's ability to achieve is to demonstrate that we genuinely care. Say, "I know your assignment is difficult, but I have confidence in you," or "Let me know what I can do to help you. I know you can do this." This is what Jesus Christ did. He showed his love through his actions and then commanded that we "love one another" as he loved us (see John 13:34). As John the Beloved teaches: "My little children, let us not love in word, neither in tongue; but in deed and in truth" (1 John 3:18).

So how did Christ demonstrate his love in his interviews? Consider the one where he met with someone we know only as "the woman at the well": "Now Jacob's well was there. Jesus therefore, being wearied with his journey, sat thus on the well: and it was about the sixth hour. There cometh a woman of Samaria to draw water: Jesus saith unto her, Give me to drink. (For his disciples were gone away unto the city to buy meat.) Then saith the woman of Samaria unto him, How is it that thou, being a

Jew, askest drink of me, which am a woman of Samaria? for the Jews have no dealings with the Samaritans" (John 4:6–9).

To better understand how much love Jesus showed this woman simply by speaking with her, we need to put the interview into historical context. There was a rift between the Jews and the Samaritans that went back for centuries. In about 720 B.C. the Assyrians had conquered the Northern Kingdom of Israel, capturing many of the inhabitants and forcing them to relocate to Babylon and live in exile.

Assyrians repopulated the empty towns and farms with people from other countries: "And the king of Assyria brought men from Babylon, and from Cuthah, and from Ava, and from Hamath, and from Sepharvaim, and placed them in the cities of Samaria instead of the children of Israel: and they possessed Samaria, and dwelt in the cities thereof. And so it was at the beginning of their dwelling there, that they feared not the Lord: therefore the Lord sent lions among them, which slew some of them" (2 Kings 17:24–25).

To avoid what they believed was divine punishment for not worshipping the geographical God of their new country, these occupiers of Samaria incorporated elements of the Jewish faith into their pagan religion and intermarried with the remaining people of Israel, horrifying the Jews. After the Babylonian captivity ended, returning Jews shunned those who, in their view, had misappropriated their homelands and religion. Samaritans later built their own temple on Mount Garizim. This further offended the Jews who felt that the Samaritan temple inappropriately mimicked the practices of the temple in Jerusalem. In the early decades of the first century, the relationship between the two groups arguably reached its lowest depth when some Samaritans desecrated the Jewish temple at Passover with human bones to enflame their cultural and religious enemies.

For a Jew at the time of Jesus to interact with a Samaritan was unthinkable. The two groups had an antipathy that rivaled that in the contemporary era of the Bosnian Serbs and Muslims or the Catholics and Protestants of Northern Ireland. The several-hundred-year-old rift is evidenced in the worst possible insult a group of Jews could think of to hurl at Christ when he once offended them by his teachings: "Then answered the Jews, and said unto him, Say we not well that thou art a Samaritan, and hast a devil?" (John 8:48).

When Jesus asked the woman at the well for a drink, he broke generations of cultural taboos. To even acknowledge her would have offended some Jews, who would have walked hours out of their way just to avoid Samaritan settlements. But to ask her for a drink of water, and thereby interact with her, was simply startling. And this was only the beginning. To help her get what she needed to be successful and happy in life, he offered her something far more precious than a drink. He offered the enemy of his people the gospel:

> Jesus answered and said unto her, If thou knewest the gift of God, and who it is that saith to thee, Give me to drink; thou wouldest have asked of him, and he would have given thee living water. The woman saith unto him, Sir, thou hast nothing to draw with, and the well is deep: from whence then hast thou that living water? . . . Jesus answered and said unto her, Whosoever drinketh of this water shall thirst again: But whosoever drinketh of the water that I shall give him shall never thirst; but the water that I shall give him shall be in him a well of water springing up into everlasting life. The woman saith unto him, Sir, give me this water, that I thirst not, neither come hither to draw. (John 4:10–11, 13–15)

Jesus agreed to share his living water, inviting the woman to get her husband and return that he might teach them both: "Jesus saith unto her, Go, call thy husband, and come hither. The woman answered and said, I have no husband. Jesus said unto her, Thou hast well said, I have no husband: For thou hast had five husbands; and he whom thou now hast is not thy husband: in that saidst thou truly. The woman saith unto him, Sir, I perceive that thou art a prophet. Our fathers worshipped in this mountain; and ye say, that in Jerusalem is the place where men ought to worship" (John 4:16–20).

At this point in the interview, Christ shows more love. Although he demonstrates that her weaknesses and sins have been revealed to him (as with the woman caught in the very act of adultery whom he saved from stoning), he does not condemn her. Neither does he offer reproach for her being argumentative, even after she, perhaps in embarrassment at having her past revealed, provokes him with a matter of contention that had divided the Jews and Samaritans for ages (the location of the true temple). Jesus refuses to engage in argument. He refuses to judge. He refuses to be caught up in the prejudice and rancor of his people. Instead he lovingly offers the best gift he can: preaching about the kingdom of God, unreservedly, and without restriction, implicitly treating the woman as if she were a member of his own people.

When the disciples happened upon Jesus speaking with the Samaritan woman they were surprised: "And upon this came his disciples, and marvelled that he talked with the woman: yet no man said, What seekest thou? or, Why talkest thou with her?" (John 4:27).

We have no record of Christ ever getting his drink of water. We know, however, that the woman drank the living water along with others she brought to be taught by Christ.

Those we interview should feel our love for them also. We demonstrate this not only by our warm and supportive words, but, as Jesus did, by offering respect, kindness, and our full confidence that the interviewee can accomplish what is necessary regardless of their station or credentials.

HOW TO ASSIGN NEW STEWARDSHIPS

Let's take a moment to discuss interviews where the leader issues a new assignment. Perhaps the most instructive example for how to do this properly is recorded in the tenth chapter of Matthew, where Jesus gives the twelve apostles their commission: "These twelve Jesus sent forth, and commanded them, saying, Go not into the way of the Gentiles, and into any city of the Samaritans enter ye not: But go rather to the lost sheep of the house of Israel. And as ye go, preach, saying, The kingdom of heaven is at hand. Heal the sick, cleanse the lepers, raise the dead, cast out devils: freely ye have received, freely give" (Matthew 10:5–8).

WHEN ASSIGNING NEW ROLES AND RESPONSIBILITIES:

1. Define clear expectations for the role. Answer the question, "How would a person in this role know whether they were being successful or not?" to the satisfaction of the new role holder
2. Provide all necessary training
3. Identify potential challenges
4. Share as much of the "what," "how," and "why" of the assignment as appropriate. Identify available resources
5. Show your confidence
6. Use boundary conditions to empower

Figure 11-2: Tips for Assigning New Stewardships

GIVE CLEAR EXPECTATIONS

Note that his instruction about their new assignment is clear and highly detailed. Jesus didn't just say: "I'd like you to do something. Please _____. Will you accept?" Rather, he tells them where they will go, what they should teach, what their specific responsibilities entail, and offers some advice on how to do it. But that's not all:

> Provide neither gold, nor silver, nor brass in your purses, Nor scrip for your journey, neither two coats, neither shoes, nor yet staves: for the workman is worthy of his meat. And into whatsoever city or town ye shall enter, inquire who in it is worthy; and there abide till ye go thence. And when ye come into an house, salute it. And if the house be worthy, let your peace come upon it: but if it be not worthy, let your peace return to you. And whosoever shall not receive you, nor hear your words, when ye depart out of that house or city, shake off the dust of your feet. Verily I say unto you, It shall be more tolerable for the land of Sodom and Gomorrha in the day of judgment, than for that city. (Matthew 10:9–15)

If leaders follow this leadership model from Jesus, they will learn that providing such detail to a new steward helps them match or supersede the expectations of their leaders. It also allows these new stewards to move forward with a clear direction and boundaries, instead of getting lost or overwhelmed with their new responsibilities.

PROVIDE TRAINING

He next provides specific training to them about how to do the assignment—including how to prepare and conduct themselves. He tells them what to do if things are going well, and what to do when they are not. But that's not all:

> Behold, I send you forth as sheep in the midst of wolves: be ye therefore wise as serpents, and harmless as doves. But beware of men: for they will deliver you up to the councils, and they will scourge you in their synagogues; And ye shall be brought before governors and kings for my sake, for a testimony against them and the Gentiles. But when they deliver you up, take no thought how or what ye shall speak: for it shall be given you in that same hour what ye shall speak. For it is not ye that speak, but the Spirit of your Father which speaketh in you. And the brother shall deliver up the brother to death, and the father the child: and the children shall rise up against their parents, and cause

them to be put to death. And ye shall be hated of all men for my name's sake: but he that endureth to the end shall be saved. But when they persecute you in this city, flee ye into another: for verily I say unto you, Ye shall not have gone over the cities of Israel, till the Son of man be come. (Matthew 10:16–23)

After decades of working with Fortune 100 companies and government agencies, we have learned that a lack of training is often a root cause for underperformance. Well-intended leaders, burdened with crushing responsibilities and schedules often feel that they can't afford the time or expense to provide training to those within their stewardship. This is a mistake. Training is a *pay me now or pay me later* proposition. To avoid future costly mistakes, reduce the ramp-up time required until someone is fully productive and ensure that desirable behaviors and cultural norms are perpetuated—proper training is a wise investment. I still remember the training I received as a new production manager with Procter & Gamble. I was fresh from college, with little real-world experience. My mentor developed a six-week training program for me with specific tasks and sign-off requirements that taught me the technical, safety, and regulatory systems of the plant. I interviewed my team members and plant managers and staff leaders to learn from them and understand their expectations. That commitment on the part of P&G to provide that level of training meant a great deal to me, and provided a foundation for success in my role for which I am still grateful to this day.

SHOW CONFIDENCE

Jesus goes on to warn the apostles of potential challenges with the assignment and helps them understand how to address those challenges. In the next nineteen verses he teaches key doctrine that will help them overcome their concerns and ultimately be successful. He expresses his confidence in them. He then concludes by sharing the blessings that will come to them and the faithful people they serve:

He that findeth his life shall lose it: and he that loseth his life for my sake shall find it. He that receiveth you receiveth me, and he that receiveth me receiveth him that sent me. He that receiveth a prophet in the name of a prophet shall receive a prophet's reward; and he that receiveth a righteous man in the name of a righteous man shall receive a righteous man's reward. And whosoever shall give to drink unto one of these little ones a cup of cold water only in the name of a disciple, verily I say unto you, he shall in no wise lose his reward. (Matthew 10: 39–42)

Think about what has been demonstrated by Jesus so far about preparing people for a new assignment. We don't even know if this account is complete, but it has already shown that leaders need to **1** clarify the assignment (in detail), **2** identify the necessary preparations/prerequisites for success, **3** establish performance expectations, **4** provide whatever tools/processes/methods/equipment are required and train people how to use them properly, **5** teach the skills required for the assignment, **6** identify required measures to take when problems/emergencies occur, **7** identify key challenges that will be faced and teach how to act in these circumstances, **8** express confidence, and, **9** explain the potential blessings/rewards for good performance. When Jesus Christ called and trained his apostles, he went far beyond what happens in many of our interviews to share new assignments. He offers a detailed explanation of the "what," much of the "how," and definitely the "why" of the assignment. Can we do less?

BOUNDARY CONDITIONS

Despite the specificity used in commissioning the apostles, however, note that Jesus allows them to exercise their own decision-making for the execution of their assignments. He tells them, for example, to go to the Gentiles. But he allows them to decide who should go, what cities to visit, and when they should leave. I have called this technique "boundary conditions": a method for clarifying expectations that allows others sufficient autonomy to generate a high level of personal commitment to their tasks that only comes from personal participation in the decision-making process.[3] In this example, Jesus establishes the boundary condition of preaching to the Gentiles, but he allows his followers to determine the specifics of execution within those boundaries. To generate the highest levels of motivation, commitment, and enthusiasm in followers, leaders should wisely follow Christ's example in this regard.

SUMMARY

Stewardship interviews are an important tool of leadership—assuming the stewardship has been given as Christ did it, with all of the specificity, training, and empowerment necessary for the other person to be successful in their new assignment.

Neither formal nor informal interviews need to be lengthy, but they should be regular, and five powerful leadership practices can help them be optimal. Those tips include: **1** prepare for the interview beforehand, **2** provide time for interaction, **3** let them do most of the talking, **4** respect personal will, **5** show Christlike love, and **6** use boundary conditions to empower others.

In the final lesson, let's review the competencies of Christlike leadership and discuss what may be the most important quality of those who strive to follow Christ's leadership example: shepherding.

NOTES

1.   William G. Dyer, "Personal Concern: A Principle of Leadership," *Ensign*, August 1972, accessed February 23, 2015, http://www.lds.org.

2.   Spencer W. Kimball, "Jesus: The Perfect Leader," *Ensign*, August 1979, accessed January 16, 2015, http://www.lds.org.

3.   Kimball Fisher, *Leading Self-Directed Work Teams* (New York: McGraw-Hill, 2000), 169–71.

Inasmuch as ye have done it unto one of the least of these my brethren, ye have done it unto me. (Matthew 25:40)

LESSON 12
BE A GOOD SHEPHERD

In this twelfth and final leadership lesson from the life of Jesus Christ, we will discuss what many believe to be his most powerful leadership competency of all: shepherding. Following the pattern established by Jesus Christ, let's open the discussion of shepherding with a story.

SHEEPHERDING AND SHEPHERDING

While I was in high school, my parents sold our home in Salt Lake City and bought a historical old farmhouse in Draper, Utah, when the town was still what would be considered a rural community. On the farm stood chicken coops and a large barn, and there was plenty of room to keep horses, have a large garden, and store my father's burgeoning collection of classic automobiles to be restored.

When we moved into the house, my parents negotiated with the previous owners to keep some of the artifacts from the original owner, J.R. Allen. I still chuckle when I think about some of the framed sheep photos that hung in the house when I was a teenager. They sported a turn of the nineteenth-century formality, with long-haired sheep looking as though they were posing for the photographer (see Figure 12-2).

Allen had been a sheep man, and had been quite famous for his prize-winning animals, including his sheep dogs, which had apparently been recognized for their superb sheepherding prowess. I heard some of the old-timers in town speak in almost reverent tones of the way the well-trained Allen dogs of long ago could form the sheep into tightly bundled groups, and drive them safely to any intended destination. The dogs could bark and heel-nip the sheep into submission, protecting them from coyotes and cougars during their long grazing drives to and from the nearby hills.

Figure 12-2: Some of the sheep of J.R. Allen

The summer after our move, I participated as one of a small group of boy scouts in a special friendship tour organized by the Boy Scouts of America. Our group of mostly Jewish boy scouts represented troops from across the Nation who traveled as U.S. ambassadors to Israel. During our six-week trip, we camped with Israeli scouts and toured Israel, roaming around the brown, rolling hills of the country in a lumbering bus. At one point of the tour, I noticed a group of sheep, and was surprised to see them attended by a long-robed shepherd carrying the same sort of curled wooden crook I had seen in New Testament paintings. As I watched, the shepherd turned his back to the sheep and appeared to leave them. Based on what I thought I knew about sheep, I assumed he had recklessly abandoned his responsibility. He casually strode off down the road, alone.

But then something interesting happened. Gradually the sheep lifted their heads from grazing, noted the shepherd's absence, and then followed after him, quickly closing the gap between them and their leader.

I had believed that without the aid of dogs, the shepherd would have to shout, or wave his crook, to get the sheep's attention, finding a way to push them ahead of him down the dusty road if he wanted them to move. He proved me wrong. There was no barking or heel-nipping involved.

And the shepherd led from the front, instead of pushing the sheep ahead of him.

This experience has served as metaphor for our firm, a sort of parable if you will, about the difference between good leaders and great ones. Mareen and I often use it in our leadership training to show that it takes a lot of patience, trust, and courage to be a shepherd.[1]

The approaches of the two leaders are very different. The sheepherder uses coercion, pushing, and force. He or she has good intentions, and often successfully protects his or her charges from outside threats. But the sheepherder leads from behind (without setting a visible example of how the sheep can move themselves), seldom trusts that the flock will move without his or her prodding, and uses methods that create dependence on the leader, not self-reliance.

Alternatively, the shepherd respects free choice and teaches his or her charges to be self-reliant. Had the sheep in the example above not been lovingly taught and cared for, they probably would have scattered, as I feared they would. But when properly taught and trusted, the charges of a good shepherd will choose to follow him or her willingly if the direction is a good one. See Figure 12-3 for a summary of differences.

	SHEEPHERDERS	SHEPHERDS
ILLUSTRATIVE METHODS	Barking, heel-nipping, pushing, prodding, ordering, forcing	Teaching, training, trusting, caring, loving, offering choices
POSITION RELATIVE TO THE FLOCK	Behind: believes the sheep need to be pushed. Worries that trust is risky. Thinks you can't keep your eyes on the sheep unless you are behind them. Believes it is more important to focus on avoiding past problems than looking to the future	In front: trusts that if the sheep are properly taught that they will choose to follow the right. Respects free will. Thinks you can't keep your eyes on the road ahead unless you are in front. Sees the need of leading out and setting an example
OUTCOMES	Creater leader-reliance	Creates self-reliance

Figure 12-3: Sheepherders versus Shepherds

THE HIRELING VERSUS THE SHEPHERD

Christ further refines this point in the parable of the hireling versus the shepherd. In John 10 we read:

> I am the good shepherd: the good shepherd giveth his life for the sheep. But he that is an hireling, and not the shepherd, whose own the sheep are not, seeth the wolf coming, and leaveth the sheep, and fleeth: and the wolf catcheth them, and scattereth the sheep. The hireling fleeth, because he is an hireling, and careth not for the sheep. I am the good shepherd, and know my sheep, and am known of mine. As the Father knoweth me, even so know I the Father: and I lay down my life for the sheep. (John 10:11–15)

Several points from this account deserve elaboration. Jesus notes that he—as the good shepherd—is fully committed, not like others who see leadership as only a job. Someone who only leads for money (or for that matter, for prestige, guilt, peer pressure, or anything other than genuine caring for those within his or her stewardship) will run away at the first sign of danger (or difficulty, or inconvenience, or whenever something more interesting comes along). A good shepherd both knows the sheep and is known by them. This can only occur through an investment of time. Can you really know someone who is merely a casual acquaintance? Can they really know you?

BECOMING A SHEPHERD LEADER IN MODERN ORGANIZATIONS

The challenge associated with truly becoming a shepherd leader is this: contemporary organizations are often built on the assumption that the ideal leadership model is more akin to sheepherding than shepherding. The hiring process is geared to recruiting hirelings not shepherds. Management policies reinforce barking and heel-nipping. Pay systems favor short-term gains over more difficult to measure long-term ones, which nearly always means that leading from the front (instead of pushing from behind) will be seen as risky—because it takes far more time to train others than to dictate to them.

The modern shepherd leader often finds himself or herself in the same place as Jesus Christ did, setting an example of leadership that runs counter to long-established cultural and organizational norms. The bad news is that shepherding behavior is often seen as aberrance and is therefore threatening to many organizations. As I have written elsewhere, this triggers a response similar to one found in the human body.[2] Much as the immune system attacks anything in the body that is foreign—even if the aberrance is good, as in the tendency for the body to reject organ transplants—organizations will often attack and attempt to destroy anything different.

The good news? Shepherd leaders, in my decades of experience in management development, outperform hireling leaders in the long run. If they can survive, they can serve as an example that can be so powerful that they can change long-established organizational norms instead of conforming to them. They can also change families, government agencies, schools, churches, and even nations.

SUMMARY

Perhaps the most important leadership competency displayed in the stories of Jesus Christ is shepherding. By following his enduring example as the good shepherd we can learn to love those we serve without reservation and lead instead of pushing others. Shepherd leaders use education and persuasion instead of barking and heel-nipping. They avoid the timid behavior of the hireling or the aggressive nature of the sheepherder.

Jesus Christ is an exemplar, scholar, believer, reprover, disciple, teacher, and shepherd, and by following him we can improve our leadership ability to help those we serve accomplish magnificent things. If you'd like some practical project ideas on how to apply the twelve leadership lessons from the life of Jesus Christ to your leadership responsibility in your organization, community, or home, consult the appendix.

NOTES

1. Kimball Fisher, *Leading Self-Directed Work Teams* (New York: McGraw-Hill, 2000), 117–19.
2. Kimball Fisher, "Teams and the Bottom Line," accessed April 9, 2015, http://www.thefishergroup.com.

LAST THOUGHTS

The leadership ministry of Jesus Christ is remarkable for many reasons. One reason is the incredible breadth of his skills, which ranged from the intense emotional and physical power of righteous indignation required of him to cleanse the temple, to the sensitive tenderness necessary for healing a sick child or raising the dead. He could confound the best educated and most powerful Pharisee and Sadducee with a story, or teach with such powerful simplicity that the weak and unschooled could understand complex doctrine about the kingdom of God. He lifted the weary and comforted the down-trodden. He calmed the blood lust in a mob with a whispered question. He healed those that raised weapons against him. He converted his enemies. He both loved and chastened his friends.

He is also remarkable because he was consistent. We see no leadership mistakes, no lapses of judgment, no selfish inclinations, no cowardliness, no exploitation of others, no awkward missteps, no corruption through absolute power. Unlike so many other celebrated leadership heroes of the past who often displayed extraordinary competence in some things, he appears to have displayed it in *all* things.

A SUMMARY OF CHRIST'S ATTRIBUTES AND LEADERSHIP COMPETENCIES

He displayed virtue, temperance, godliness, knowledge, faith, hope, humility, righteousness, obedience, diligence, courage, patience, charity, and brotherly kindness. And in this book I have tried to illustrate his leadership abilities in several key areas including the seven competencies listed on pages 16 and 17. Christ was an exemplar, scholar, believer,

113

reprover, disciple, teacher, and shepherd—aspects of which we should consider incorporating into our own leadership practice. After serving in the leadership development industry for many decades, I feel confident that applying Christlike leadership practices in our homes, organizations, schools, communities, and governments would improve leadership practices and effectiveness everywhere.

But be ye doers of the word, and not hearers only, deceiving your own selves. (James 1:22)

APPENDIX
APPLY THE 12 LEADERSHIP LESSONS

In this appendix I'll suggest some examples of practical projects for applying each of the twelve leadership lessons from the life of Jesus Christ to your own responsibilities. This application project idea is consistent with the way Jesus taught, and I believe it will help you become a more effective leader in your organizations, communities, and homes.

LESSON 1: BE VISIONARY

Organization: Identify a significant area of your stewardship and create a vision statement for it that answers the questions: **1** "What do we need *to be* to reach our full potential?" **2** "Where do we currently fall short of this vision?" and **3** "How do we get from where we are today to where we need to be in the future?" Find appropriate ways to begin sharing your vision and building momentum for change.

Community: Participate with others to create a shared vision for a part of your community where you serve as a leader. On large sticky notes, have each participant write down a short statement that captures what they would most like to see the group become. Then post the notes on a wall and have participants work together to assemble the notes into groups of similar ideas. Discuss the "aspiration groupings" and together create a summarizing statement for each one that the participants agree should be included in a vision statement. Ask a volunteer to take the statements and craft a compelling vision document that he or she will share in your next meeting. At that meeting, fine-tune the statement wording, and have everyone affix their names to an inspirational paragraph you post on your website, or have them sign a statement you hang in your office.

Home: Create a family mission statement. Older children can participate by answering the question: "What is most important to our family?"

LESSON 2: BE A SERVANT LEADER

Organization: Write a job description for your leadership position that is consistent with the traditional "dominion" or "control paradigm" view of management. Then write a description from the perspective of the "servant leader" or "commitment paradigm" perspective. Analyze the differences and determine which parts of your role need to be transformed so you can become more of a servant leader. Discuss this analysis with your own leader and see if you can get agreement and support to make the necessary changes.

Community: Campaign for leaders and changes that are more consistent with servant leadership than dominion. To get some feedback on your own leadership style, conduct an anonymous opinion survey with questions that will help you determine whether you are perceived as more of a servant leader or a dominion leader.

Home: Select an activity or decision that you would normally organize or dictate in a controlling manner. You might consider, for example, how chores are supervised, or how household budgets are developed and discussed, or how household rules are enforced. Then, determine how to do an activity as a servant leader, instead. Do it that way and observe the reactions of other family members.

LESSON 3: BE A GOOD EXAMPLE

Organization: Recognize that you are always an exemplar of something. Conduct an anonymous survey to determine what kind of example you are setting. Ask questions such as: "Identify the critical priorities for our organization as demonstrated by your leader's personal example," "List three areas where your leader's example exceeds and three areas where your leader's example falls short of stated organizational values or goals," and/or "If the only direction you received was to follow the example set by your leader, what would you assume you are supposed to do?"

Community: Evaluate your most important areas of responsibility. For the top three areas, identify how you could display your commitment to this responsibility. For example, instead of just saying you value helping the less fortunate, you could volunteer to work in a soup kitchen. Prior to doing this you might announce to those you work with, "I'm trying to set a better example at (fill in the blank). I'd like you to watch what I do and let me know if there is anything I need to improve so that my actions are consistent with what I say is important."

Home: As a family, determine an area you would like to improve in. Discuss what example the parent(s) would have to set to help the family make the desired improvement.

LESSON 4: BE INSPIRING AND MOTIVATING

Organization: Sit down with one of your team members who is having problems motivating himself or herself and discuss what you can do to create an environment that will help.

Community: Identify something that must be done but for which there has been insufficient political or social motivation. Discuss with a group of volunteers what information would be necessary to create that motivation and with them find a way to disseminate the information effectively. For example, if you believe that schools are underserved by parents because the parents don't know what they can do, start up a blog for your school with a calendar that lists volunteer activities and projects.

Home: Discuss as a family something that you need to do together. Decide on a reward or tracking system that would encourage everyone to pull together to accomplish the desired goal.

LESSON 5: EMPOWER TEAMS

Organization: Examine your organization to locate an extraordinary team and determine with them what makes them so successful. Have them develop a presentation that captures their learnings and then provide an opportunity that allows them to share the presentation appropriately with other teams and team leaders. For example, if one of the things that makes the team so successful and empowered is a unique method of information sharing via the company intranet, invite the teams to participate in a webinar where the unique information sharing template is demonstrated and offered to others.

Community: Identify a committee that is struggling to be successful and find out what lack of support, guidance, or other resource prevents them from accomplishing what they need to accomplish. Help the committee put together a plan to resolve the deficiency.

Home: Ask family members what parents can do to better empower children to make good choices. Enact at least one of the suggestions.

LESSON 6: DELEGATE

Organization: Create a list of your leadership responsibilities. Select the responsibilities that can be delegated and create a delegation worksheet as follows: **1** In the first column list the responsibilities as specifically as possible. For example, rather than write "administrative tasks," write "schedule vacations." Instead of "meetings," write "facilitate weekly staff meeting." **2** In the second column write the name of an individual to whom that specific task should be delegated. **3** In the third column record the date by which you plan to delegate the task. **4** In the fourth column list the special support or training that needs to be given to the individual so that the delegation will be successful. **5** In the fifth column list the success criteria (the answer to the question: "What specifically would the person need to do to demonstrate that he or she has mastered this delegated assignment?"). When you scan down the columns you will be able to create a delegation plan that includes the appropriate team and individual preparations necessary for effective delegation.

DELEGATION WORKSHEET

Key Responsibility	Delegated to Whom	Delegation Date	Training and Support	Success Criteria

Community: Select someone you work with who would benefit from a development opportunity. Pick a project that will help them develop new skills, including some elements of your responsibilities that will need to be delegated. Craft the project so that it includes meaningful assignments, share it with them, and explain how you will be available to train and support them to be successful.

Home: Determine an activity or decision that is normally done by you to be delegated to someone in the family who is ready to assume it (e.g., planning a vacation, preparing some meals, selected areas of shopping/

budgeting). Before turning the responsibility over to the person, carefully train them how to do it properly. If they make an honest mistake, rather than taking back the responsibility, discuss what was learned by the mistake and encourage the individual to keep at it. Let them know by your actions that you believe they are capable and trustworthy.

LESSON 7: RESOLVE CONFLICTS

Organization: Ask two teams or individuals in conflict to sit down with you or a neutral third party to attempt to resolve their dispute. Start by having them identify a mutually agreed reason why it is worth the effort to resolve the conflict. This reason might be something as simple as, "we have to work together better to make the organization successful," or "we don't like the way it feels to avoid each other." After hearing from both parties about their perspectives and concerns, try to determine the root cause for the conflict and stay in the room until you come up with a plan to try to address the disagreement. If, for example, the root cause for the conflict is a lack of communication between two shifts, institute a brief shift overlap meeting to provide an opportunity to do "pass downs" of key information from one shift to the other.

Community: Try a facilitated process to resolve a conflict between two organizations as follows: **1** Have people from group A share their perspectives about the issue *without any interruptions from group B*. **2** Have group B summarize what they heard from group A without any editorial comment or disagreement. **3** Ask group A if group B's summary is accurate. If not, continue the process until it is. **4** Complete the same steps for the other group. At the end of the presentations (once everyone believes their position is understood by the other side) put together a mutually agreed-upon resolution plan.

Home: Identify a disagreement or misunderstanding that could turn into a conflict and help family members talk it out before it escalates. Be sure to help each party identify and articulate what expectations were violated.

LESSON 8: AVOID UNRIGHTEOUS DOMINION

Organization: Complete the self-assessment about unrighteous dominion written in the chapter. If you have a high level of trust within your team, share your assessment with them and ask for their honest opinion of what they think about it. Ask for examples when they disagree with your assessment. Put together a personal leadership improvement plan based on their feedback.

Community: Conduct a culture assessment by asking your team to pretend that they are cultural anthropologists who live 100 years in the future. Assume that your organization/committee is perfectly preserved as it is today, and that the anthropologists are charged with describing what your culture must have been like, based only on the artifacts they uncover. Have them list the artifacts (policy manuals, constitutions, organizational charts, offices, furniture, website, social media records, etc.) they found, and what these artifacts tell them about your organization's dominion or commitment-based attributes. Also ask what the artifacts convey about dominion or servant-based leadership roles and which of the cultural artifacts they want to keep or eliminate.

Home: Be introspective about whether your parenting behaviors exhibit any qualities of unrighteous dominion. If married, discuss this together with your spouse. Plan how to change the incorrect behavior. You may consider seeing a family therapist for assistance.

LESSON 9: BE A TEACHER

Organization: Create a development plan for each of your team members. Remember to include the key skills and knowledge required for each person individually, considering both present and future needs. When the learning needs have been identified, determine how to best meet them, and which needs will be taught by you. Then create a development schedule jointly with the individuals involved to enact the plan.

Community: Have the team brainstorm the most important things for them to learn in order for the organization they work in to be successful. Pick one of the topics you have expertise in and create a meaningful activity to teach it. Remember that many things are taught more effectively through an experiential activity (field trip, special project, hands-on training, etc.) than a classroom presentation. For example, if the organization is a youth football team you are coaching, and the topic is safety, invite a manufacturing rep from a helmet company to come and put on an engaging presentation on concussion avoidance and treatment.

Home: Pick an evening to do something educational together. After you go to the activity (concert, lecture, game, show, church, special meeting, library, etc.) sit down and discuss it together in a way that is appropriate for the ages of your family members.

LESSON 10: CORRECT OTHERS PROPERLY

Organization: Review your best and worst examples of annual reviews from your previous boss(es) and answer the question: "What made some of these discussions about things I needed to improve helpful, while others were not?" Based on what you learn, modify your upcoming performance appraisal/improvement discussions appropriately. Two or three months after your appraisals, meet with the team members who are not demonstrating progress on the desired improvements to determine what you need to do differently as a leader to help them.

Community: In order to help a non-paid volunteer in an organization you lead improve his or her performance, meet with him or her and have a loving discussion about how you can help. Since you probably will have neither a carrot (reward) nor a stick (punishment) that you can use to help him or her become motivated to improve, express your appreciation for whatever positive contribution he or she has made, and together discuss the questions: "What do we want in this organization that we don't already have?" and "How do we want to be remembered after our service has been completed?" to help the individual find a motivating reason to act differently.

Home: Think about a correction you did with a family member that didn't go as well as you hoped it would. Using things you learned in this chapter, apologize to the person, and try to do it again differently.

LESSON 11: BE A GOOD STEWARD

Organization: Have stewardship interviews with each member of your team and jointly create (or modify) a job description with each employee to represent the discussions. Then have a team meeting with everyone to discuss the position accountabilities. Have each person review his or her description and answer questions. After that, discuss the joint responsibilities (things like safety, housekeeping, customer responsiveness, admitting when they make mistakes, making deadlines, communicating effectively, etc.) shared by each member of the team. If a joint accountability document doesn't exist, create one of those as well, and have everyone on the team affix their signature to it.

Community: Ask team members to each create a list of things he or she believes he or she is accountable for. Have a virtual or face-to-face group discussion, giving each person an opportunity to present his or her list. After each presentation, encourage team members to ask questions and make suggestions. At the end of the meeting you'll have a renegotiated list of accountabilities (by person) that should cover all essential activities and responsibilities.

Home: Create some family rules or chores together and discuss how everyone can help everyone else live by your agreements. Decide on a special treat or activity that you will have if everyone keeps the rules/does the chores for an agreed amount of time.

LESSON 12: BE A GOOD SHEPHERD

Organization: Ask yourself honestly if you care about everyone in the organization you lead. If you don't, evaluate what it is that prevents you from having this feeling (knowing people better? learning how to care about people who are different than you? overcoming feelings of superiority? etc.), and put together an appropriate plan to do what is necessary to create this authentic concern. If necessary, speak to your human resources department to employ coaching, mentoring, university courses, or other professional resources to assist you to make progress in this regard.

Community project: Find a community project that truly inspires you and volunteer to serve others meaningfully without receiving any compensation for your time or efforts. Encourage others to join with you to make a difference in these people's lives.

Home: Identify someone in your family that you believe you need to improve your relationship with. If you are unable to make progress through your own efforts, go to counseling together with a mutually respected psychological or spiritual advisor and commit to a relationship improvement plan.

ABOUT THE AUTHOR

Kimball Fisher has spent thirty years as a consultant specializing in training leaders and teams to be more effective. He has worked with about twenty percent of the Fortune 100 corporations—places like Apple Computers, Bristol-Myers Squibb, Capital One, Chevron, GE Capital, Hewlett-Packard, Intel, McDonald's, Microsoft, NBC, Nike, and Weyerhaeuser—teaching leadership and team skills across the Americas, Europe, Scandinavia, Asia, and Africa. He's also worked with several universities, churches, and government organizations including the IRS, the U.S. Departments of Treasury and Agriculture, and the staff office of the U.S. Senate. He is the author/co-author of the business best sellers *Leading Self-Directed Work Teams* and *The Distance Manager* (with Mareen Fisher).

Fisher received a leadership scholarship from BYU, where he graduated with a Bachelor's degree in Humanities and a Master's degree in Organizational Behavior. He was the first recipient of the prestigious William G. Dyer Award for outstanding contributions to the field of management.

He and his wife live in Portland, Oregon. You can reach him at www.kimballfisher.com.